Urban Politics and Decentralization

Urban Politics and Decentralization

The Case of General Revenue Sharing

Richard L. Cole
George Washington University

David A. Caputo
Purdue University

Lexington Books
D.C. Heath and Company
Lexington, Massachusetts
Toronto   London

Library of Congress Cataloging in Publication Data

Caputo, David A   1943-
    Urban politics and decentralization.

    1. Intergovernmental   fiscal   relations—United   States.
2. Decentralization in government—United States. 3. Municipal
government—United States. I. Cole, Richard L., joint author.
II. Title.
HJ725.C36   336.1'85   74-4485
ISBN 0-669-93039-3

Published simultaneously in Canada.

Printed in the United States of America.

International Standard Book Number: 0-669-93039-3

Library of Congress Catalog Card Number: 74-4485

For Alice and Pam

Contents

List of Tables   ix

Preface   xiii

Acknowledgments   xix

Chapter 1   **Urban Politics and Decentralization: The Issues**   1

Introduction   1
Historical Context   1
Decentralization and the Political Process   6
Conclusion   11

Chapter 2   **The History of General Revenue Sharing: Its
                 Philosophical and Fiscal Justification**   17

Introduction   17
Early Examples   17
Categorical Grant Programs   18
The State and Local "Fiscal Crisis:" 1950-1972   19
Revenue-Sharing Proposals   22
President Nixon and Revenue Sharing   29
Alternatives to General Revenue Sharing   30
Conclusion   32

Chapter 3   **The State and Local Fiscal Assistance Act of 1972**   39

Introduction   39
President Nixon's Commitment to General Rev-
    enue Sharing   39
The Legislative Process: 1969-1972   41
General Revenue Sharing and the New
    Federalism   53
Conclusion   61

Chapter 4   **General Revenue Sharing and City Expenditure
                 Decisions**   67

Introduction   67
Expenditure Decisions   70
Revenue-Sharing Expenditure Decisions and City
    Size, Type, and Region   73

Municipal Reform and Revenue Sharing Expenditures 80

Revenue Sharing and Demographic Variables 84

Conclusion 90

Chapter 5   **Program Consequences of General Revenue Sharing: Policy Innovation, Citizen Participation, and Taxing Efforts** 95

Introduction 95

Revenue Sharing and Program Innovation 95

Citizen Participation and the Allocation of Revenue-Sharing Funds 98

Impact of Revenue Sharing on Categorical Grant Programs and Municipal Taxing Levels 103

Attitudes of Municipal Officials toward General Revenue Sharing 108

Conclusion 112

Chapter 6   **Partisan Politics and Coalition Building: The Future of General Revenue Sharing** 121

Introduction 121

Recipient Satisfaction 124

Conclusion 141

Chapter 7   **General Revenue Sharing: The New American Revolution** 147

Introduction 147

Empirical Findings 147

Theoretical Interests 150

General Revenue Sharing: Evaluation and Assessment 153

Appendix A   **Research Strategy and Questionnaires** 161

Appendix B   **Restrictions on Expenditure of General Revenue Sharing Funds** 169

Appendix C   **Reform Scale** 171

Indexes 173

About the Authors 181

List of Tables

1-1   Historical Development of the Urban Population in the United States   2

2-1   Trends in Economic Growth and Governmental Finances: 1957-1966   20

2-2   Local Government Expenditures for Various Functions: 1966   21

3-1   General Revenue-Sharing Funds Received by State Governments: 1973   54

3-2   General Revenue-Sharing Funds Received by 50 Largest Cities: 1973   56

4-1   Questionnaire Response Rates   69

4-2   Prior Budgetary and General Revenue-Sharing Expenditures (%) in Cities over 50,000   71

4-3   General Revenue-Sharing Expenditures and City Size   75

4-4   General Revenue-Sharing Expenditures and City Type   77

4-5   General Revenue-Sharing Expenditures and Region   78

4-6   General Revenue-Sharing Expenditures and Form of Government   82

4-7   General Revenue-Sharing Expenditures and Municipal Reformism   83

4-8   Mean Income and General Revenue-Sharing Expenditures   85

4-9   Non-White Population and General Revenue-Sharing Expenditures   87

4-10   Population Change and Revenue-Sharing Expenditures   89

5-1   Use of Revenue Sharing for New and Existing Programs, by Form of Government   97

5-2   Use of Revenue Sharing for New and Existing Programs, by Environmental Factors   98

5-3   Use of Revenue Sharing for New and Existing Programs, by Function   99

5-4   Public Hearings and the Allocation of Revenue-Sharing Funds   100

5-5   Public Hearings and the Allocation of Revenue Sharing,

	by Political, Environmental, and Demographic Characteristics	101
5-6	Effect of Public Hearings on Revenue-Sharing Allocations	102
5-7	Use of Revenue-Sharing Funds for OEO and Model Cities Activities	105
5-8	Use of Revenue-Sharing Funds for OEO and Model Cities Activities, by Political and Environmental Characteristics	106
5-9	Impact of General Revenue Sharing on Municipal Taxing Levels	108
5-10	Impact of General Revenue Sharing on Municipal Taxing Levels, by Political, Demographic, and Environmental Characteristics	110
5-11	Effect of General Revenue-Sharing Funds on Total Federal Funds for Urban Areas	112
5-12	Effect of General Revenue-Sharing Funds on Total Federal Funds for Urban Areas, by Political and Environmental Characteristics	113
5-13	Respondent Satisfaction with General Revenue Sharing	114
5-14	Consequences of Revenue Sharing: A Summary of Overall Trends, by Categories of Cities	116
6-1	Respondent Satisfaction with General Revenue Sharing and City Size, Region, and Type	126
6-2	Respondent Satisfaction with General Revenue Sharing and Form of Government	128
6-3	Respondent Satisfaction with General Revenue Sharing and Structural Organization	130
6-4	Respondent Satisfaction with General Revenue Sharing and Demographic Variables	132
6-5	Effect of General Revenue-Sharing Funds on Total Federal Funds, by City Size, Region, and Type	134
6-6	Effect of General Revenue-Sharing Funds on Total Federal Funds, by Form of Government	138
6-7	Effect of General Revenue-Sharing Funds on Total Federal Funds, by Structural Reformism	139

6-8   Effect of General Revenue-Sharing Funds on Total Federal Funds and City Socio-Economic Characteristics   142

7-1   Expenditure and Impact Consequences of General Revenue Sharing: A Summary Table   149

7-2   Complaints Handled by the Office of Revenue Sharing   152

7-3   Office of Revenue Sharing Employment   152

Preface

As passed by the Congress and signed into law by President Nixon in October 1972, the State and Local Fiscal Assistance Act (General Revenue Sharing) is to return approximately $30.2 billion to state and local governments during its five-year life. In terms of monetary outlay alone, as has often been observed, the program rivals the man-on-the-moon project of the 1960s. However significant its fiscal impact, the political consequences of revenue sharing are equally profound. For the last thirty to forty years, some would argue, the changing nature of the American federal system has been characterized by increasing national involvement in and dominance over state and local affairs. This is particularly true, it has been suggested, during the period of "creative federalism" (generally associated with the Kennedy and Johnson Administrations) in which the number of grant-in-aid programs made available by the national government to states and localities increased from just over 100 in 1960 to nearly 600 by 1972. In dollar amounts, this meant an increase of from $7 billion to almost $30 billion. More important is the shift in "emphasis" of many of those grant programs enacted in the 1960s. Whereas grant-in-aid programs prior to the 1960s usually did not involve expressly stated national purposes, many of those enacted since 1960 were conceived as a means by which the national government could achieve *its* objectives.

Revenue sharing, according to some, has ushered in an era of "new federalism," one which is designed to reverse the flow of power and authority to Washington and, as former President Nixon has stated, to return decision-making authority to the states, the communities, and the people. When signing the revenue-sharing bill in October 1972, President Nixon declared that the "New American Revolution" is underway.

This is a study that focuses on general revenue sharing and its implications for metropolitan America. Our concern is with the impact of general revenue sharing in its broadest fiscal, legal, social, and political contexts; however, it should be clear to the reader that we concentrate especially on the *political* and *policy* aspects of general revenue sharing. Thus, while such important issues as the impact of general revenue sharing on taxing status and the distribution of revenue-sharing funds to various functional categories are not ignored, we are equally interested in such issues as the political and social factors associated with revenue-sharing expenditures; the extent to which city official officials have permitted and encouraged citizen participation in general revenue-sharing decisions and the impact of such participation; the effect of general revenue sharing on policy innovation; those groups most affected by general revenue sharing; and those coalitions likely to oppose and support general revenue sharing in coming legislative debates. Thus, our central focus concerns the question of which groups are affected and how they are affected as decision making is decentralized. General revenue sharing, we believe, provides an ideal opportunity to examine the well-established theory that changing the locus of decision making may affect the outcome of the decision itself.

Nature of the Study

This study presents in a single volume a discussion of the history and development of the revenue-sharing philosophy (Chapter 2), an in-depth examination of the bill as passed in 1972 (Chapter 3), and an analysis of the fiscal and political impacts of the expended funds (Chapters 4, 5, and 6). Our impact data are drawn from two national surveys of chief executive officers in every American city over 50,000 and from an extensive data file containing political, demographic, and fiscal information on these same cities. Our two surveys were conducted in January 1973 and January 1974. Thus, the officials were responding after having received approximately half of the total $30.2 billion in general revenue-sharing funds. Although funding limitations and time restrictions limited our surveys to cities over 50,000, it should be noted that these cities receive approximately 60 percent of the total amount of general revenue-sharing funds allocated to American cities.

Chapter 4 examines in greater detail the response rate to our survey; here, it should be mentioned that in each year our responses amounted to just over 50 percent of the total number of cities surveyed. After utilizing a variety of checks and analytical routines, we have not been able to detect any consistent bias in the responding cities. In addition, expenditure responses to our survey parallel very closely those of all cities in this size category as reported in official Office of Revenue Sharing publications. In general, we believe our sample fairly reflects the expenditure patterns and attitudinal characteristics of the chief executive officers of all cities in this size category.

Why Study General Revenue Sharing?

Although the $30.2 billion of general revenue-sharing funds to be distribted obviously is a large amount of money, the question of why the impact of general revenue sharing on urban America is an important focus of study might legitimately be raised. After all, one-third of the funds go to the states and the rest is to be distributed among more than 38,000 units of local government. Thus, it might be assumed, the impact of revenue sharing in any single city is likely to be negligible.

While there may be some truth to this argument, our position of course is that revenue sharing is worthy of intense and in-depth analysis. In the first place, revenue-sharing funds do amount to a significant portion of the budget of many American cities. In fact, general revenue-sharing funds amount to 10 percent or more of the budgets of the following major cities: San Antonio, New Orleans, Phoenix, Pittsburgh, Portland, Oklahoma City, Louisville, Miami, El Paso, Birmingham, and Tampa. Those large cities in which revenue sharing funds amount to almost 10 percent of their budgets include Chicago, Houston, and Detroit. In spite of its wide distribution, then, revenue sharing is having a significant fiscal impact on even some of America's largest cities.

In addition, general revenue-sharing funds represent, at least in theory, "new money"—that is, money unencumbered by previous commitments. As students of the budgetary process are well aware, uncommitted funds can be far more significant than might be indicated by their proportion to the total budget alone.

Revenue sharing also is an important topic of study because it provides a unique opportunity to urban scholars to examine how metropolitan areas respond to change. How do cities react to new resources, and what are the political and demographic variables associated with those responses? These topics are considered in our analysis. In addition, general revenue sharing may be renewed in the next two years. Intensive policy analysis, such as ours, may provide a unique perspective for the decision maker interested in policy-related research investigating the policy impact of the program.

Most important, as discussed above general revenue sharing is worthy of study because of the philosophy of which it is a key element—the philosophy of decentralization. The theoretical questions involving decentralization are explored in Chapter 1. In addition, as discussed in the following chapters, general revenue sharing was only one element in President Nixon's overall "New Federalism" domestic plans. While significant portions of these proposals were not approved by Congress prior to his resignation, general revenue sharing has now been in existence long enough to begin to provide answers to the central question of our study: "who gets what, when, and how as decision making is decentralized?"

How to Study Revenue Sharing

An issue prompting considerable debate among those interested in the general revenue-sharing legislation concerns the method by which the impact of general revenue sharing can best be studied. The primary methodological issue concerns what has been called the "fungibility" of general revenue-sharing money. By this, it is meant that because of the nature of the funds, the "real" impact of revenue sharing may never be accurately assessed. For example, a city official may report spending large portions of general revenue-sharing funds for parks and recreation; however, those revenue-sharing expenditures may have freed money that would have been spent for parks and recreation anyway, and those freed funds may have then been allocated to another area, perhaps public safety. Thus the real impact of revenue sharing in this instance, it is pointed out, may actually be in the area of public safety although the official reported spending revenue sharing for parks and recreation. Some have even suggested that for political reasons public officials may purposefully misrepresent their revenue-sharing expenditures.

While we recognize that these possibilities exist, we believe that the problem may not be quite as severe as some have suggested. In the first place, city officials are required by law to keep an accurate account of revenue sharing's planned and actual uses, to periodically provide these reports to the Office of Revenue Sharing, and to publish these reports in their local newspapers. These measures, we believe, provide some "check" on revenue-sharing expenditures. Some cities, in fact, have gone so far as to prepare separate budgetary statements for publication and distribution detailing the precise expenditures of revenue-sharing money. Perhaps the most compelling evidence that officials do attempt to report accurately the use of revenue-sharing funds, however, is provided by an examination of their responses. The usual assumption is that officials may be reluctant to report large expenditures for such programs as public safety (law enforcement and fire prevention) for fear of the adverse reaction among socially oriented groups, both in and out of Congress. However, we found that cities do report the largest proportion of revenue-sharing funds being allocated to public safety areas—this in contrast to what some would judge to be in their best interest.

We believe that to a large extent the evidence indicates that officials have honestly reported the expenditure of general revenue-sharing funds and that to a considerable degree these reports are an accurate measure of the impact of revenue sharing in the various communities. At the same time, we strongly suggest that it is only through the comparison of a variety of studies utilizing different methodological techniques that a final assessment of the impact of general revenue sharing can be made. Our study, we believe, contributes one perspective to this important area of metropolitan policy analysis, and we anticipate repeating our survey on a year-to-year basis throughout the life of general revenue sharing.

Chapter 1 considers the important theoretical and policy questions related to general revenue sharing and outlines the hypotheses to be examined throughout the book. The following chapters examine in detail the fiscal, social, and political impacts of general revenue sharing for urban

America. Our intention is to answer as many questions as possible and to raise others that need additional investigation and research.

Acknowledgments

The authors of this study wish to express their gratitude to many who have assisted in the various stages of the preparation of this book.

In the first place, we are grateful to Purdue University, the Purdue Research Foundation, and The George Washington University for individual research grants, which greatly facilitated our work. In addition, the research assistance of Paul Anderson, Greg Freeman, and Lisa Hoffman—all of whom possess and displayed abilities characteristic of the most skilled policy researchers—is gratefully acknowledged. Our students at Purdue and George Washington continue to be a source of inspiration and constructive criticism.

We wish to express our appreciation to Diane Amos, Rita Lynch, and especially Dotty Eberle who skillfully and without complaint typed the various (and sometimes endless) revisions and who performed their tasks in spite of considerable time constraints and competing demands.

Of course, we owe a special debt of gratitude to those city mayors, city managers, and finance officers responding to our surveys. We trust that their tolerance and patience has not been abused.

Christopher and Elizabeth were quite understanding of the frequent absences and long nights of intense work by their father. Most especially, we wish to thank our wives, Alice and Pam, who graciously and unselfishly shared considerable amounts of their time with this project. To them, this book is dedicated. Of course, we alone assume full responsibility for the points developed and the ideas presented in the following pages.

Urban Politics and Decentralization: The Issues

Introduction

Urban America has received increased and widespread attention from both the general public and policy makers in the last 15 years. Concern with various urban "problems" and the overall quality of life in urban America has often dominated public interest and resulted in numerous attempts to improve or ameliorate conditions. This concern with urban America was reflected in the debate and discussion concerning the initial general revenue-sharing legislation and will most certainly dominate the discussion as general revenue sharing is considered in the future. The relationship between general revenue sharing and several important theoretical and conceptual points are examined in this chapter.

To begin with, the United States has experienced and continues to experience an increase in the percentage of its population residing in metropolitan areas. Table 1-1 indicates the growth of the urban population and the rapid concentration of population in the urban areas of the United States. This certainly helps to explain the increased concern over solutions and improvements appropriate to urban life. Coupled with this growing concentration of urban population has been a general awareness that many local units of government, for a variety of reasons, have failed to meet the needs of rapidly growing populations in many areas. General revenue sharing is usually seen as an alternative to past attempts to deal with meeting these local problems. It is for this reason that the study of the political effects of general revenue sharing is so critical. If research dwells only on the fiscal aspects of the legislation, the important power and resource distribution questions associated with the general revenue-sharing concept and actual programs are ignored. While we do not ignore the fiscal aspects of general revenue sharing, this book concentrates and places emphasis on the political and social implications of the general revenue sharing program. This chapter, then, considers the important theoretical and empirical questions associated with the study of general revenue sharing.

Historical Context

Certainly one of the most debated topics in American political theory is the

1

Table 1-1
Historical Development of the Urban Population in the United States

	Total Population (000)	Total Urban Population (000)	Percent Urban
1910	91,972	41,999	45.7
1920	105,711	54,158	51.2
1930	122,775	68,955	56.2
1940	131,669	74,424	56.5
1950	150,697	89,749	59.6
1960	179,323	125,269	69.9
1970	203,212	149,325	73.5

Source: Table No. 18, U.S. Bureau of the Census, *Statistical Abstract of the United States: 1973* (Washington, D.C.: Government Printing Office, 1973), p. 18.

nature of federalism in the United States. Persistent and often lively scholarly and political debate has characterized this discussion.[1] Simply stated, the United States, as a federal system, is comprised of two sovereign levels of government: the governments of the 50 states and the national government. The Constitution, of course, establishes the basic framework for this system;[2] however, scholars have long recognized that the definition of federalism is flexible and that various political and legal interpretations of federalism have prevailed at differing periods of the nation's history.[3] These various interpretations of federalism have been symbolically characterized by such slogans and phrases as "dual federalism," "cooperative federalism," "creative federalism," and "new federalism." Throughout American history, the final authority has been the Supreme Court. A review of the various decisions reached by the Court indicates the varying judicial interpretations of the nature of federalism that have prevailed at different points in time.[4] Certainly the Civil War can be seen as a clash over conflicting interpretations, and the long judicial struggle characterizing the 1930s and the New Deal was largely due to a debate over the appropriate role of the national government.[5]

Numerous scholars have presented their perspectives on the relationship between the national and state governments. Probably the most influential view in recent years is that offered by Morton Grodzins who maintained the "layer cake" theory of American federalism was inappropriate and that in fact federalism in the United States more closely resembled a "marble cake."[6] Proponents of the layer cake theory held that one level of government was indeed more powerful than the other, but more importantly, they stressed the fact that the functions and responsibilities of the two layers were indeed separate and easily divisible.[7] There was little recognition of "shared" functions and the attempt was usually to classify all programs according to which "layer" of government was responsible for that program. Grodzins maintained that federalism in the United States more nearly resembled a marble cake in that many functions and responsibilities were shared or performed by both the national and state governments.[8] Grodzins and others, such as Daniel Elazar, have supported their position by pointing out the important and necessary roles played by the various state governments throughout American history.[9] Throughout this consideration, concern is often voiced over the possible domination by the national government in areas and over functions that are largely state functions or that are best shared.

Related to these contending views of American federalism are two important points. The first is that the Constitution fails to recognize or to grant power to units of government other than those at the national and state levels. In addition, the Tenth Amendment specifically reserves all undelegated powers to the states.[10] Thus, local governments are legally viewed as creations of the states they are in and are subject to periodic changes and political shifts in their powers and responsibilities. In essence then, the specific legal status of local governments in the 50 states differs in terms of type of, number of, and specific responsibilities assigned by state constitutions or statutes. The powers and responsibilities of local governments differ markedly throughout the United States as a result of each state's ability to determine which and how powers are to be delegated to local units. Despite the legal aspects of local governmental units, there has been extensive and increasing contact among the local units and both the state and national governments in recent years. It is precisely in these relationships that the greatest change in American federalism has occurred in the last 25 years.[11] Thus, a much broader definition of intergovernmental relations must be used that includes local-national and local-state relationships as well as state-national relationships.

For a variety of reasons, the national government has increased its activity in America's urban centers since 1949. Beginning with the 1949 Housing Act and continuing into the 1970s, the national government has indeed become an active participant in most cities where attempts to deal with pressing problems have been made. [12] Throughout this period, the key questions have involved:

1. What is the relationship between the national and state governments in administering and implementing the programs?
2. What is the relationship between the national and local governments with respect to the programs?
3. What is the relationship between the individuals affected by the various programs and the governmental units involved?

Perhaps the above points are best illustrated by briefly considering the recent "War on Poverty."

Brought on by a variety of political factors, the Economic Opportunity Act of 1964 was structured so that local poverty programs were directly financed by the national government.[13] The role of state governments in the program was limited and initially the active participation of elected local officials was not required.[14] The poverty program was an attempt to use national government funds to solve or ameliorate local problems. Certainly the most controversial aspect of the war on poverty was the community action portion of the legislation, which authorized and established local agencies to administer the war on poverty with the "maximum feasible participation" of groups affected by the programs.[15] While the confusion and disagreement resulting from this legislative requirement cannot be explored here, it does illustrate the importance of structural arrangements in determining policy making.

The "War on Poverty," as well as urban renewal and other national programs, which were common in the 1960s (usually referred to as categorical grant and grant-in-aid programs), required recipient units of government not only to develop specific plans and to gain approval for them from national program officials but also, in most cases, to contribute some local "matching" funds in return for federal funds. The national government, through its legislative and fiscal control of the programs, determined what the specific program eligibility requirements were to be as well as the funding level of the programs. Except in isolated cases, these programs received appropriated funds on a fiscal year basis; thus, the amount of funds available in a given fiscal year was affected by a wide variety of political and economic forces and subject to the annual budgetary review conducted by Congress. Chapters 2 and 3 of this book discuss the specific criticisms of the categorical grant and grant-in-aid programs; the point to be made here is that general revenue sharing is indeed a departure from the prior approach used to finance programs and represents a possible change in the basic nature of intergovernmental relations in the United States.

The original general revenue-sharing legislation of 1972 appropriated funds for a trust fund that would guarantee a set amount of funds through 1976. More importantly, there were no eligibility requirements; two formulas were used to distribute the funds to the more than 38,000 general purpose units of government in the United States. Federal reporting requirements were minimal and the recipient units of government had few restrictions placed on how the funds could be spent. General revenue sharing was unique in that the emphasis was now on "freeing" recipient units of government by providing resources with few restrictions to deal with problems affecting them.

This shift raises several important questions concerning fiscal and political accountability. Two aspects of the accountability question must be considered. One involves the expenditure of funds by the unit of government that has not raised those funds. Should expenditure decisions in these cases be left entirely to the participants in the local decision-making process, or should there be restrictions and/or guidelines set by the governmental unit that raised the money and allocated it to the recipient units? Before dismissing this point as trivial, it should be recalled that the use of federal funds was responsible for major, if not always totally beneficial, changes at the local level. Excellent examples of this point exist in the various considerations given to the urban renewal and war on poverty legislation.[16] The point is clear: Is it acceptable for one unit of government to expend funds raised by another governmental unit? Although federal requirements as to how general revenue-sharing funds are to be spent are minimal, [17] does this fact make accountability at the recipient unit's level any different than if there were greater requirements? Obviously, some decision makers have raised this point. Most notable among these has been Congressman Wilbur Mills who, prior to his supporting general revenue sharing, regularly asked whether indeed it was constitutionally correct for the unit of government responsible for raising the money to transfer expenditure of the funds to units of government at another level.[18] This is an important question in the nature of federal fiscal relations in the United States and will continue to be vigorously debated and discussed.

The accountability question has another aspect to it. If governmental units expend funds raised by another governmental unit, what, if any, obligations or requirements can the unit responsible for the raising of the funds place on the unit spending the funds? In short, if the recipient unit uses its funds to obviate a decision by the higher unit, can it be penalized or have its funds eliminated? In the case of general revenue sharing, the restrictions on the recipient units of government are minimal.[a] These restrictions involve a series of priority expenditure categories for local units of government, a nondiscrimination clause, and compliance with the Davis-Bacon legislation.[19] The practical result is that general revenue-sharing funds can be spent with maximum discretion at the local level. The accountability questions were clearly resolved in favor of granting increased discretion to the local units of government over how the funds were to be spent.

While the accountability problem and the questions it raises deserve consideration, more important is the perspective on American federalism that general revenue sharing may provide. The question is basic: Is general revenue sharing the beginning of a trend towards greater power for local units of government by providing them with otherwise unavailable and largely unrestricted resources raised by the national government? If this is in fact the case, then constitutional scholars will need to develop new

---

[a]See Appendix B for a discussion of the restrictions on the expenditure of general revenue sharing funds.

theoretical descriptions of American federalism as these changes are experienced. There is little doubt that this aspect of general revenue sharing will receive the attention it deserves, but one point should be made clear. If in fact the funds do permit local units of government more discretion than former national programs, it is reasonable to expect that the programs and recipients benefitting from the funds may be different from those who benefitted from other programs. This question needs empirical investigation, but one cannot and should not assume that a change as basic as general revenue sharing will not lead to different policy decisions and impacts.

Another interesting aspect of urban politics pertinent to revenue sharing concerns the topic of policy and program innovation. On the one hand, it might be argued that the city manager form of government, with its emphasis on centralization and professionalization, would facilitate rapid and innovative decision making. On the other hand, it might be argued that because of their emphasis on planning and rationality, reform cities will be slower in allocating "new" sources of funds. The fact of the matter, as discussed in Chapters 4 and 5, is that very little is presently known about which political and structural variables are associated with rapid and innovative decision making at the local level and the data that are available are often conflicting. General revenue sharing provides an ideal opportunity to examine these relationships.

Related to the theoretical aspects of questions dealing with American federalism and general revenue sharing are the empirical questions raised by general revenue sharing. These are considered in the next section.

Decentralization and the Political Process

While the ultimate effect general revenue sharing will have on the nature of American federalism must await additional time and study, The State and Local Fiscal Assistance Act of 1972 presents political scientists with a unique and excellent opportunity to investigate both the policy outcomes and the policy impacts of general revenue sharing as one example of decentralized decision making. This section, then, raises the important analytical and empirical questions that the study of general revenue sharing may shed some light on. The "who gets what, when, and how" questions are among the most important issues to be raised about general revenue sharing.

Policy outcomes are the decisions reached as to how revenue-sharing funds have been utilized and the relationships of those decisions to a variety of political and demographic variables. This should certainly be an important aspect of any research dealing with general revenue sharing and builds on two previous themes characterizing prior urban research.

The first of these themes is perhaps one of the more interesting debates of the recent past. It involves the contention that expenditure decisions are influenced by a variety of factors but that the underlying cultural traits of a governmental unit's citizenry are major factors in these expenditure patterns. The contribution of James Q. Wilson and Edward C. Banfield in developing this theory should not be underestimated.[20] In their *City Politics* and subsequent writing, Banfield and Wilson have contended that socioeconomic class and other cultural variables have a measurable impact on governmental decisions.[21] Banfield and Wilson, drawing upon a variety of historical sources—notably Richard C. Hofstadter's, *Age of Reform*[22]—hypothesize that cities with largely middle-class populations will favor policy beneficial to the city as a whole and are concerned with such issues as honesty, impartiality, economy, and efficiency. On the other hand, their thesis would argue that cities reflecting an immigrant or lower-class ethos would oppose those policies because they contradict the basically private and neighborhood orientation of their inhabitants.

Responding to the ethos theory and the ensuing debate it prompted, researchers began to concentrate on the policy outcomes of various cities and factors affecting or determining those outcomes. There has been persistent criticisms of both the underlying theoretical assumptions and empirical verification of the "ethos concept."[23] Raymond Wolfinger and John Osgood Field concluded that ". . . the ethos theory clearly needs a good deal of modification. Whether a revised version will have much explanatory power remains to be seen."[24] Prompted by this debate, Robert L. Lineberry and Edmund P. Fowler considered the impact political structural variables had on policy outcomes.[25] They concluded: "The translation of social conflicts into public policy and the responsiveness of political systems to class, racial, and religious cleavages differ markedly with the kind of political structure. Thus, political institutions seem to play an important role in the political process—a role substantially independent of a city's demography."[26] If the Lineberry and Fowler contention is correct, it should also be applicable to the general revenue-sharing decision-making process. Thus, the following hypotheses could be investigated:

H_1: *Reform cities will exhibit different general revenue-sharing expenditure patterns than partisan cities.*

H_2: *Reform cities will place greater emphasis on general revenue-sharing expenditure decisions and categories that favor the "community interest" rather than the narrow interests of a small or geographically confined group.*

H_3: *Reform cities will reach general revenue-sharing expenditure decisions more rapidly than partisan cities due to the decreased role of political interaction.*

The impact of structural variables can be readily investigated utilizing general revenue-sharing data. One would expect that expenditure decisions would reflect the hypothesized variation if indeed political structure had an impact on policy outcomes. The role of political structure in determining policy outcomes needs renewed consideration by those interested in policy research as it may provide important information as to the structural variables that impede or promote access to and influence over the policy-making process.

The relationship of political structure and policy outcomes has been challenged by researchers who maintain that "environmental" variables are far more influential in determining policy outcomes.[27] The relationship between a variety of personal socioeconomic variables and expenditure decisions by various governmental units have been extensively investigated. In fact, this research has been definitive enough to permit Brett W. Hawkins to conclude that "many recent studies of state and local policy outputs . . . suggest that policies are more a product of environmental than system factors and that environment can only be ignored at the cost of adequate explanation."[28] Hawkins' observation appears applicable, and full credit must be given to the research done by Thomas R. Dye,[29] Terry N. Clark,[30] Harvey Brazer,[31] and others[32] who have investigated the impact environmental variables have on expenditure decisions. It would be logical to assume a similar relationship between general revenue-sharing decisions and such environmental variables. The following hypotheses are consistent with prior research findings and can be investigated by utilizing general revenue-sharing data:

H_1: *Regional location will have a decided impact on general revenue-sharing expenditure decisions. For instance, Southern cities will spend less on social services than cities in the Northeast.*

H_2: *The larger the population, the more diverse the demands for public services and the greater the demand for increased levels of services.*

H_3: *Large cities–those over 250,000 population– will spend a larger proportion of their general revenue-sharing funds for police and fire protection than will cities of smaller size.*

H_4: *Cities with larger percentages of non-white and low-income populations will have greater percentage expenditures of general revenue-sharing funds for health and social services than those cities with a lower percentage of non-white and low-income populations.*

H_5: *Cities with large "middle-class" populations will have greater percentage expenditures of general revenue sharing funds for parks and recreation, libraries, and educational items than will cities with small "middle-class" populations.*

The list could go on, but the point should be clear. General revenue-sharing decisions permit the re-examination of the relationship between expenditure decisions and environmental variables. If consistent patterns are prevalent, major conclusions concerning the underlying relationship are then possible. Through careful analysis of general revenue-sharing decisions, substantial new evidence can be brought to the debate concerning the impact of environmental variables on expenditure decisions.

A second aspect of decentralization and the political process involves more qualitative conclusions concerning who benefits or loses from the various policy outcomes. In short, what is the impact of the policy outcomes on various groups?

Political scientists and sociologists investigating the community decision-making process often have arrived at differing characterizations of it. Three need to be briefly reviewed here. The first is the notion that community decision making is usually dominated by a small socioeconomic elite that obtains its desired policy outcomes at the expense of the general public's good. This conclusion is usually associated with the research conducted by sociologists and especially the community-oriented research of Robert S. and Helen M. Lynd[33] and Floyd Hunter.[34] Those holding this theory contend that economic power is the basis for political power and that the economic elite, through economic sanctions and rewards, controls the political process.

This view has been challenged by Robert Dahl in his major study of New Haven, Connecticut.[35] Dahl contends that city political processes are more accurately described as having few individuals with direct influence participating in the policy process, but with many individuals having indirect influence over the policy process by their active use of the vote and other participatory possibilities.[36] The debate between Dahl and his proponents and the sociologists and political scientists who contend economic elites dominate has been directed towards both substantive conclusions and the methodologies used to reach those conclusions.[37] The pluralist-elitist debate often centered on what city and issues were investigated and the preconceptions brought to the research by the investigator.[38]

While Dahl's research was generally accepted by those associated with the pluralist school of thought, considerable opposition to it came from a variety of sources. On the one hand, critics such as Jack Walker maintained that the type of and roles of participation acceptable to Dahl and other pluralists were in fact largely elitist oriented and failed to provide individual citizens with adequate participatory possibilities.[39] Another criticism involved the "non-issue" and mobilization of bias theories and was put forth by Peter Bachrach and Morton S. Baratz.[40] Building on an earlier argument by E.E. Schattschneider,[41] Bachrach and Baratz contended that elites may be so powerful that they can covertly control which issues are placed in the public arena.[42] Thus, the study of overt issues or issue areas ignores this possibility and may in fact lead to unwarranted conclusions concerning the "openness" of a political system. Bachrach and Baratz contend that if in fact issues were kept off the decision agenda in cities studied by the pluralists, the conclusions reached by the pluralists were invalid.

Revenue-sharing research has a unique contribution to make to this debate. By investigating the expenditure decisions reached by cities and the manner in which those decisions were reached, researchers may in fact cast considerable light on the preceding discussion. For instance, if the research indicates the decision process did not involve the public or that cities failed to respond to the needs of a significant portion of their population, one would have evidence to support those who claim local decision making is in fact a very closed process and that individuals and broad community interests often have little direct impact on the ultimate outcome. If research indicates public interaction and decisions reflect the public's concern, then the pluralists will have evidence to support their contention.

Even more important, such investigation will permit conclusions pertaining to the impact of the decentralization of the decision-making process. As Chapters 2 and 3 indicate, this is obviously one of the key rationales for the general revenue-sharing legislation and a point often advanced by its prominent supporters such as former President Richard M. Nixon.[43] The contention of those supporting general revenue sharing is clear; return the necessary resources to the local decision-making unit and that unit will reach decisions most reflective of local needs and preferences. However, it is clear that the decentralist rationale means much more than simply altering the locus of decision making. As Schattschneider pointed out in his classic study of American politics, changing the locus of decision making may drastically alter the decision reached itself.[44] The recent history of the United States indicates, Schattschneider argued, that as the arena of decision making is enlarged, decisions favorable to the socially and politically disadvantaged are more likely to be reached. Likewise, as the decision-making arena is narrowed, decisions favorable to the status quo are more likely. As Schattschneider notes, "throughout American history tremendous efforts have been made to control the scope of conflict" and he suggests that "perhaps the whole political strategy of American local government should be re-examined in [this] light."[45] Undoubtedly, Schattschneider would have argued that the debates surrounding the passage of general revenue sharing could best be understood from this perspective.

In recent years, racial and economic minorities have tended to look to the national government to provide them with policy solutions to their needs. Certainly racial desegregation is such an example. Also, the various categorical and grant-in-aid programs in the areas of poverty and housing involve efforts by the national government to require local compliance with national regulations if federal funds are to be received. General revenue sharing permits the establishment of local priorities by local officials and reduces the nationally established requirements for the receipt of federal funds. Thus, according to traditional theories of federalism, it would be reasonable to expect that revenue sharing, a measure returning a considerable amount of spending discretion to states and localities, would result in conservative status-quo-oriented decisions. The money, it would be predicted, will be spent largely for "hardware" items to the exclusion of social service and welfare areas. At the same time, it is true, as Suzanne Farkas has pointed out, that the past several years have witnessed the organization and "politization" of a number of previously politically disadvantaged groups in the urban setting.[46] This organization, Farkas contends, might well be used to prevent reactionary policies and might partially offset the conservative biases usually found in localized decision making. To the extent that these predictions are true, it is obvious that our traditional theories and expectations of federalism and its impact on decision making need re-examination and re-evaluation. The data presented in this book permit the initial steps in that direction.

Conclusion

This chapter illustrates the theoretical and empirical importance of general revenue sharing. Developed during an important domestic era, the research concerning general revenue-sharing outcomes and their possible impacts need to be fully explored. Our attempt throughout is to accomplish four goals:

1. To examine the political and social forces leading to the passage of general revenue sharing.
2. To describe as fully as possible the revenue-sharing decisions reached by city governments over 50,000. (This is done by discussing the various expenditure decisions reached in 1973 and 1974.)
3. To explain as fully as possible the reasons for these expenditure decisions. (For example, what are the demographic and structural impacts of these decisions? The nature of such impacts and the policy implications are then fully considered.)
4. To provide a full understanding and evaluation of general revenue sharing within its policy context and with full consideration of its impact on American politics and federalism. (Here we are interested primarily in the critical question of "who wins and who loses" as decision making is decentralized. Description and explanation are supplemented with

the theoretical and empirical developments general revenue sharing may prompt.)

An understanding of these objectives is essential to a full understanding of our basic intentions. Before moving to a description of the general revenue-sharing decisions in cities over 50,000, it is important to understand fully the legislative background and political forces affecting the passage of general revenue sharing. Chapters 2 and 3 consider these points.

Notes

1. James Bryce, *The American Commonwealth* (New York: The Macmillan Company, 1916): Edward S. Corwin, *The Twilight of the Supreme Court* (New Haven: Yale University Press, 1934); Jane Perry Clark, *The Rise of a New Federalism* (New York: Russell and Russell, 1965, first published in 1938); George C. S. Benson, *The New Centralization* (New York: Farrar and Rinehar, 1941); Arthur W. Holcombe, *Our More Perfect Union* (Cambridge, Mass.: Harvard University Press, 1950); Carl Becker, *The Declaration of Independence* (New York: Alfred A. Knopf, 1958); Daniel J. Elazar, *The American Partnership* (Chicago: University of Chicago Press, 1962); William H. Riker, *Federalism: Origin, Operation and Significance* (Boston: Little Brown & Co. 1964); Morton Grodzins, edited by Daniel J. Elazar, *The American System* (Chicago: University of Chicago Press, 1966); Aaron Wildavsky (ed.), *American Federalism in Perpsective* (Boston: Little Brown & Co., 1967); James Sundquist and David Davis, *Making Federalism Work* (Washington: The Brookings Institution, 1969); and Michael D. Reagan, *The New Federalism* (New York: Oxford University Press, 1972).

2. See Article I, Section 8; Article II, Section 2; Article III, Section 2; and Article IV of the United States Constitution for a discussion of the responsibilities and duties of the national and state governments.

3. For a useful summary of one aspect of this debate, see Daniel J. Elazar, "Federal-State Collaboration in the Nineteenth Century United States," *Political Science Quarterly* 79 (June 1964), pp. 248-81.

4. Ibid.

5. Alexander H. Stephens, *A Constitutional View of the War Between the States* (Philadelphia, 1868); and Edward S. Corwin, *The Twilight of the Supreme Court* (New Haven: Yale University Press, 1934).

6. For a brief description of Grodzins point of view, see *The American System,* pp. v-vi.

7. See Clark, *The Rise of a New Federalism.*

8. Grodzins, *The American System,* pp. v-vi.

9. Ibid.; also, see Daniel J. Elazar, *The American Partnership;* and *American Federalism: A View from the States* (New York: Crowell, 1966).

10. Article X of the Amendments to the United States Constitution.

11. See Sundquist and Davis, *Making Federalism Work,* pp. 1-10 for a discussion of these changes.

12. Ibid.

13. For a full discussion of the War on Poverty, see John C. Donovon, *The Politics of Poverty* (Indianapolis: Bobbs-Merrill, 1973); Sar A. Levitan, *The Great Society's Poor Law* (Baltimore: The Johns Hopkins Press, 1969); Daniel P. Moynihan, *Maximum Feasible Participation* (New York: The Free Press, 1969); Richard L. Cole, *Citizen Participation and the Urban Policy Process* (Lexington, Mass.: D.C. Heath, Lexington Books, 1974) provides empirical evidence specifying the impact participation in poverty and other programs had on the individual.

14. See Levitan, pp. 112-8 for a discussion of the community action concept.

15. See Moynihan for a conjectural statement on the impact of citizen participation and Cole for an empirical investigation of this point.

16. See Levitan and Moynihan for a discussion of the impact of the poverty program and James Q. Wilson (ed.), *Urban Renewal: The Record and the Controversy* (Cambridge: M.I.T. Press, 1966) for a discussion of urban renewal's impact.

17. See Public Law 92-512, Sections 103, 104, 121, and 123.

18. For a discussion of Representative Mill's original proposal, see Maureen McBreen, *History of Federal Revenue Sharing Proposals and Enactment of the State and Local Fiscal Assistance Act of 1972* (Washington: Library of Congress, 1972), pp. 17-18.

19. See Public Law 92-512.

20. See Edward C. Banfield and James Q. Wilson, *City Politics* (Cambridge: M.I.T. Press, 1963) and James Q. Wilson and Edward C. Banfield, "Political Ethos Revisited," *The American Political Science Review* LXV (December 1971), pp. 1048-62.

21. Ibid., pp. 33-46, 224-42 and 1048-9.

22. Richard Hofstadter, *The Age of Reform* (New York: Alfred A. Knopf, 1955).

23. See Raymond Wolfinger and John Osgood Field, "Political Ethos and the Structure of City Government," *The American Political Science Review* LX (June 1966), pp. 306-26.

24. Ibid., p.326.

25. Robert L. Lineberry and Edmund P. Fowler, "Reformism and Public Policies in American Cities," *The American Political Science Review* LXI (September 1967), pp. 701-16.

26. Ibid., p. 715.

27. See Wolfinger and Field; John H. Kessel, "Governmental Structure and Political Environment," *The American Political Science Review* LVI (September 1962), pp. 615-20; Richard E. Dawson and James A. Robinson, "The Politics of Welfare," in Herbert Jacob and Kenneth Vines (eds.), *Politics in the American States* (Boston: Little, Brown & Co. 1965); and Thomas R. Dye, "City-Suburban Social Distance and Public Policy," *Social Forces* 4 (1965), pp. 100-6.

28. Brett W. Hawkins, *Politics and Urban Policies* (Indianapolis: Bobbs-Merrill, 971), p. 61.

29. Thomas R. Dye, *Politics, Economics, and the Public* (Chicago: Rand McNally, 1966).

30. Terry N. Clark, "Community Structure, Decision-Making, Budget Expenditures, and Urban Renewal in 51 American Communities," *American Sociological Review* 33 (August 1968), pp. 576-93.

31. Harvey E. Brazer, *City Expenditures in the United States* (New York: National Bureau of Economic Research Incorporated, 1959).

32. Alan K. Campbell and Seymour Sacks, *Metropolitan America: Fiscal Patterns and Governmental Systems* (New York: The Free Press, 1957) and Richard L. Cole, "The Urban Policy Process: A Note on Structural and Regional Influences," *Social Science Quarterly* (December 1971), pp. 648-56.

33. Robert S. Lynd and Helen M. Lynd, *Middletown* (New York: Harcourt, Brace, & Co., 1929) and Robert S. Lynd and Helen M. Lynd, *Middletown in Transition* (New York: Harcourt, Brace, & Co., 1937).

34. Floyd Hunter, *Community Power Structure: A Study of Decision-Makers* (Chapel Hill: University of North Carolina Press, 1954).

35. Robert Dahl, *Who Governs?* (New Haven: Yale University Press, 1961).

36. See Dahl's summation of this point on pp. 163-5 of *Who Governs?*

37. For a summary of the debate see, John Walton, "Substance and Artifact: The Current Status of Research on Community Power Structure," *American Journal of Sociology* 32 (January 1966), pp. 430-8.

38. See Nelson W. Polsby, *Community Power and Political Theory* (New Haven: Yale University Press, 1963).

39. Jack L. Walker, "A Critique of the Elitist Theory of Democracy," *The American Political Science Review* LX (June, 1966), pp. 285-95. See

Robert A. Dahl's, "Further Reflections on 'The Elitist Theory of Democracy'," *The American Political Science Review* LX (June 1966), pp. 296-305, for his response to Walker's critique.

40. Peter Bachrach and Morton S. Baratz, *Power and Poverty: Theory and Practice* (New York: Oxford University Press, 1970).

41. E.E. Schattschneider, *The Semi-Sovereign People* (New York: Holt, Rinehart, and Winston, 1960).

42. See the discussion of this point by Bachrach and Baratz, *Power and Poverty: Theory and Practice,* pp. 6-9.

43. Richard M. Nixon, "Revenue Sharing Public Address" (San Clemente, Cal.: Office of the White House Press Secretary, August 13, 1969).

44. Schattschneider, *The Semi-Sovereign People*.

45. Ibid., pp. 7, 9.

46. Suzanne Farkas, "The Federal Role in Urban Decentralization," in Richard Feld and Carl Grafton (eds.), *The Uneasy Partnership* (Palo Alto, Cal.: National Press Books, 1973), pp. 146-7.

The History of General Revenue Sharing: Its Philosophical and Fiscal Justifications

Introduction

Few pieces of legislation have had as interesting and controversial history as has general revenue sharing. In its various forms, revenue sharing has been advocated and supported by members of both political parties, by conservatives as well as liberals, by national as well as state and local officials, by academicians as well as politicians. It is clear that the bill, as finally passed in 1972, owed much of its format and substance to these earlier proposals as well as to particular fiscal and political circumstances of the late 1960s and early 1970s. This chapter sketches the intellectual history of general revenue sharing and focuses especially upon the important fiscal and philosophical justifications of the measure as they were advanced at the time of its adoption. An appreciation of the general revenue-sharing legislation also is facilitated by an understanding of its major alternatives. These are briefly reviewed at the conclusion of this chapter.

Early Examples

In 1964, Robert Heilbroner called revenue sharing, "a really new idea in domestic economic policy,"[1] and a decade later, following the passage of general revenue sharing, Thomas Dye commented that "revenue sharing is a true landmark in American federalism."[2] Despite the public excitement and academic interest generated by the general revenue-sharing act of 1972, it is apparent that general revenue sharing, in its broadest concepts, is in reality a very old idea in American federal relations and that examples of legislation embodying the general revenue-sharing philosophy prior to the Civil War can be found. In fact, it can be argued that legislative experiments with the general revenue-sharing concept predate the categorical grant programs that many now believe general revenue sharing may be designed to replace.

Perhaps the most interesting of the early "revenue-sharing" experiments was the Surplus Distribution Act of 1836, passed during the administration of President Andrew Jackson.[3] During Jackson's presidency, a surplus of federal funds had accumulated from the sale of public lands. In order to expend these funds, the Surplus Distribution Act provided that all money in the federal treasury in excess of $5 million be distributed among the states on the basis of each state's representation in Congress. This money was to be distributed in four installments. Although only three of these installment periods were actually met (because of the financial panic of 1837), $28 million actually was returned to the states. According to Maureen McBreen's account, most of this unrestricted money was spent by the states for educational purposes and the rest was used "to pay current expenses, to reduce state indebtedness, to build roads, bridges, canals, or to make other internal improvements."[4] Interestingly, the State of Maine made a per capita distribution of its share of the money.[5]

Although the Surplus Distribution Act may be an extreme example, it is true that the many requirements and restrictions, which later were to characterize the categorical grant-in-aid programs, were largely nonexistent prior to the Civil War. Describing the general system of federal grants-in-aid in the pre-Civil War era, one student of federalism has commented: "The federal government made little or no attempt to restrict the use of federal funds or to regulate state expenditure of federal money. There had developed no federal power to prescribe the minimum standards or even to aid in their formulation, much less to exercise any continuing power of inspection or supervision over state activities undertaken with such funds. Therefore, the early grants were gifts with few or no strings attached."[6] Clearly the mechanisms, by which funds such as those made available by the Surplus Distribution Act were allocated and expended, were very similar to those incorporated in the contemporary general revenue-sharing philosophy.

Categorical Grant Programs

However, these early "revenue-sharing" experiments were quickly abandoned. According to Jane Clark, it is widely believed that the funds were not used in the most constructive manner, and, in fact, she asserts that the states were "enticed to their destruction by squandering their patrimony, or at best [selling] it for what many people think was a mess of pottage."[7] The Morrill Act of 1862, donating lands to the states specifically for the purpose of higher education, marked a turning point in the federal grant-in-aid system, and the philosophy of unrestricted grants was dormant for over 100 years. Unlike the unconditional provisions of the Surplus Distribution Act, the vast majority of federal grants to state and local governments since the Civil War have been for specific purposes. Several excellent historical treatments of the categorical grant-in-aid programs, as they are called, are available, and an extended discussion of their development is not necessary here.[8] However, it is important to note that the key feature of these categorical grant programs is that they are made for specific and narrowly defined purposes and to one degree or another require federal approval of state and local plans and federal inspection of activities.[9] The depression years and the New Deal witnessed a tremendous proliferation of categorical grants, and it is estimated that the number of such assistance programs had reached almost 600 by 1970.[10] The areas covered by these programs include agriculture, airports, civil defense, cultural pursuits, education, fish, game and wild life, health and hospitals, housing, highways, labor, natural resources and pollution control, public works, recreation, transportation, veterans and welfare. By fiscal 1972, federal funds earmarked in this manner totaled nearly $30 billion and amounted to about 20 percent of all state and local resources.[11] Clearly, a wide variety of state and local activities have been covered by the categorical grant concept. The major distinctions between the categorical grant approach and other means of federal-local financing are discussed at the conclusion of this chapter.

The State and Local "Fiscal Crisis": 1950-1972

The 1950s and 1960s witnessed a revival of academic and political interest in revenue sharing. Revenue sharing, it seems, had something to offer those of almost every political persuasion. During this period, it is estimated that over 100 bills advocating some form of revenue sharing were introduced in the Congress.[12] For some, revenue sharing was seen as a means of reversing the flow of political power to Washington back to the states and localities; for some, it was viewed as a means of modernizing state and local governments; while others saw in it the possibility of reducing local property taxes. Undoubtedly, the most often cited justification for revenue sharing in this period, however, was what appeared to be an impending "fiscal crisis" for state and local governments.

Indeed, financial data of the 1950-1970 period did indicate serious financial problems for state and local governments. Students of local finance interpreted the data as indicating that the needs of state and local governments would outpace the growth of the gross national product, while the revenue collected by the federal government would outstrip its financial needs. Thus, many were concerned with a "fiscal imbalance" in the federal system—a situation in which state and local governments were faced with the fastest growing demands for public services but the least flexible and desirable means of raising revenue, while the resources available to the national government appeared to be in excess of its needs. For many observers, a sharing of this federal "surplus" with the local units of

Table 2-1
Trends in Economic Growth and Governmental Finances: 1957-1966

Item	1957 (Billions)	1966 (Billions)	Percent Increase 1957 to 1966	Average Annual Percent Increase, 1957 to 1966
Gross National Product	441.1	747.6	69.5	6.0
Personal Income	351.1	586.8	67.1	5.9
State and Local Governments:				
Total revenue	45.9	97.6	112.5	8.7
Revenue from own sources[a]	42.1	84.5	100.8	8.1
Revenue from federal aid	3.8	13.1	241.3	10.2
Total expenditures	47.6	94.9	99.6	8.0
Total debt	53.0	107.1	100.8	8.1
Local Governments Only:				
Total revenue	29.0	59.3	104.2	8.3
Revenue from own sources[a]	21.4	41.5	94.3	7.7
Total expenditures	31.3	61.0	96.4	7.8
Total debt	39.3	77.5	97.2	7.8

[a]Excludes federal and intergovernmental aid.

Source: *Building the American City,* Report of the National Commission on Urban Problems to the Congress and to the President of the United States (Washington, D.C.: U.S. Government Printing Office, 1968), p. 411.

government was the most logical solution. Table 2-1 compares the growth of the gross national product in the 1957-1966 decade with the increase of expenditures of state and local governments.

As Table 2-1 indicates, the gross national product and personal income had increased by about two-thirds during this decade, while the total expenditures and total debt of state and local governments had doubled. Most economists of this period saw little hope that the tendency for the needs of state and local governments to outstrip economic growth would abate.

In addition to the continued expansion of state and local service needs, many observers noted that inferior revenue-raising options were available to most local governments. In 1969, the national government received 91.9 percent of all revenue collected via the income tax; states and localities received only 8.9 percent.[13] Yet, the income tax is the most sensitive source of governmental revenue in an expanding economy. Because of its heavy reliance on the income tax, the national government can anticipate automatic higher income in tax revenues as the economy grows. State and

Table 2-2
Local Government Expenditures for Various Functions: 1966

	Percent of all Local Government Expenditures[a]	
Function	38 Largest SMSAs	All U.S. Cities
Education	38.3%	43.5%
Police Protection	11.6	9.0
Interest on General Debt	6.6	5.9
Financial Administration	6.3	6.4
Health and Hospitals	5.9	5.3
Fire Prevention	5.6	4.5
Streets and Highways	5.3	7.0
Parks and Recreation	4.4	3.3
Sewerage	2.9	2.7
Public Welfare	2.8	2.3
Refuse Collection and Street Cleaning	2.7	2.1
General Public Buildings	2.0	2.2
Water Supply	1.9	2.0
Libraries	1.4	1.3
Housing and Urban Renewal	.5	.4
Airports, Terminals, Parking	.2	.2
All Other	1.5	1.8

[a]Net of intergovernmental revenue and user charges.

Source: *Building the American City*, Report of the National Commission of Urban Problems to the Congress and to the President of the United States (Washington, D.C.: Government Printing Office, 1968), p. 410.

local governments, relying heavily on property and sales taxes, must take the politically risky course of increasing those taxes as their needs increase.[14] In addition to its taxing advantage, as pointed out by the Advisory Commission on Intergovernmental Relations, the national government enjoys another revenue-raising advantage—it is unencumbered from the problems of interlocal and interstate tax competition.[15] State and local governments, competing for business and residential growth, are understandably reluctant to increase their taxes.

It was often pointed out that compounding these problems was the fact that those areas in which state and local spending is concentrated were those in which financial needs were most likely to rapidly increase. Table 2-2 indicates the proportionate amount of funds received by each functional category of state and local spending in the mid-1960s. Those who favored the sharing of federal revenues with states and localities argued that those areas in which local units of government spent most of their money, such as education, police and fire prevention, the environment, and health and hospitals, were those areas which would be facing particularly pressing needs in the near future. According to Congressman Henry Reuss (whose revenue-sharing plan is examined below), "The shape of things to come in the major areas where local governments must play a leading role —education, public safety, health, welfare, housing, transportation, the environment, recreation, and culture—is foreboding."[16]

Thus, observers could point to severe financial problems of state and local governments during this period. Demands for state and local services were increasing, the debt of these units of government was expanding, and their sources of revenue were not keeping pace with economic growth and citizen demands. During the 1960s, the nation's urban civil disturbances emphasized the need for major programs to deal with pressing urban economic, political, and social problems. At the same time, the national government's revenue-raising techniques (individual and corporate income taxes) insured it of automatic higher revenue yields as the economy expanded. Indeed, many felt that the national treasury would soon have a surplus of funds. These data led many to conclude that state and local governments faced a severe fiscal crisis and that some sharing of national revenue was appropriate.[17] Accordingly, revenue-sharing measures were advocated by a number of Democrats, Republicans, and academicians. Those having the most direct relevance for the legislation, as finally passed in 1972, are reviewed below.

Revenue-Sharing Proposals

One of the earliest Republican advocates of revenue sharing was Melvin Laird, later to serve as a cabinet member and special advisor in the Nixon Administration. It is said that Laird's interest in revenue sharing dates back to 1946 when he was a member of the Wisconsin legislature. That year, the Wisconsin legislature adopted a plan for the sharing of state revenues with its cities and counties.[18] In 1958, as a Republican Congressman from Wisconsin, Laird introduced in the House of Representatives a bill calling for tax-sharing legislation. Commenting on his plan, which was also introduced in every session of Congress from 1958 until he left to join the Nixon cabinet, Laird stated: "This is the second half of the twentieth century. America has grown more complex; the world has grown more troubled; and the time for talk of better solutions to move our country forward has long passed. The growing public support for the principle of revenue sharing as the better way for a modern America to do things demands we move forward now."[19] Laird's proposal called for a straight 5 percent return to the states of federally collected personal income taxes. The money was to be returned to the states with no strings attached, except that an optional provision was inserted that would allow for the use of 5 percent of the sum received by each state for improving state administrative procedures. It is interesting to note that in discussing his measure in 1967, Laird acknowledged the possibility of "special revenue sharing." He believed that special revenue-sharing measures, "while not as desirable as an across-the-board revenue-sharing plan," nevertheless are "certainly steps in the right direction."[20]

In 1966, Republican Congressman Charles E. Goodell of New York also introduced a revenue-sharing proposal. Under the Goodell version, 3 percent (which was to gradually increase to 5 percent) of federal income taxes would be returned to the states. Interestingly, Goodell's proposal contained provisions for "weighting" the distribution of returned money in favor of less wealthy states as well as "pass-through" provisions by which local governments would reveive a proportion of the funds. Goodell proposed that 90 percent of the money be allocated to the states on the basis of population and that the remaining 10 percent be distributed among the 17 states having the lowest per capita income. Also, he proposed that 45 percent of the returned money be given specifically to local governments to be spent at their own discretion.[21] Thus, the Goodell proposal contained two important elements (formulas to assist least wealthy states and pass-through provisions) later incorporated in the revenue-sharing act as passed in 1972.

The Republican Party, itself, went on record as favoring revenue sharing in a 1966 report issued by the Republic Coordinating Committee entitled "Financing the Future of Federalism: The Case for Revenue Sharing."[22] In that report, the committee endorsed a plan that would return from 2 to 10 percent of personal and corporate income taxes to the states. The report recommended that the funds be used with a minimum of federal control. Also, in 1965, the Republican Governors' Association and the Ripon Society, a liberal Republican organization, endorsed the principal of revenue sharing.[23] The report, as jointly issued by these two organizations, was especially critical of the "increasingly centralized government" and viewed revenue sharing as a means by which that centralization could be reversed.

During this period, the Democratic Party, as well, responded favorably to the revenue-sharing proposal. In 1964, the platform adopted at the Democratic National Convention recommended that the federal government should consider the development of a program to share revenues with the states and localities. In his 1964 campaign, President Johnson declared his intent to carry out the revenue-sharing provisions of his party's platform and he proposed that the federal government make available to the states and localities "some part of our great and growing federal tax revenues—over and above existing aids."[24]

Probably the most often-cited revenue-sharing plan prepared by a Democrat is that proposed by Wisconsin Congressman Henry S. Reuss. The Reuss proposal is interesting because it carried with it the provision that states receiving aid must demonstrate evidence of administrative modernization. According to Reuss, his proposal was encumbered with no strings ''other than the one big initial string—that the state prepare in good faith a modern government program setting forth what it proposes to do in the years ahead to invigorate and modernize its own and its local governments.''[25] As proposed, the Reuss measure would have made $50 million available to the states for their expenses involved in planning such administrative reforms. A coordinating committee of governors would have been set up to ''screen'' reform programs and to forward to the president those proposals the committee found to reflect ''sufficient creative state initiative.'' Only those states approved by the president and the coordinating committee of governors as having prepared sufficiently creative administrative reforms would have been eligible to receive grants under the Reuss proposal. Those reforms that Reuss felt most desirable included shorter ballots, longer terms for office holders, higher paid legislators, and state-wide merit systems.[26]

According to the financial details of his plan, the Reuss proposal would have authorized the return of about $5 to $10 billion a year to the states. Reuss believed that the approval of his plan (which he called a ''domestic Marshall Plan'') would dramatically alter the future shape of federalism. The federal government, he felt, would continue its role as guarantor of civil liberties and civil rights and would continue to represent the interests of the United States in foreign and defense policies. The states, of course, would assume a renewed and invigorated role in the system. The states would not be allowed to ''wither on the vine,'' according to Reuss, but would assume a revived role. Reuss predicted that state programs so stimulated ''could offer an escape from the insolvency, the fragmentation, the ultra localism, the poor services, the unbalanced communities, and the citizen apathy of local government today.''[27] Unquestionably, the most distinctive aspect of the Reuss proposal was its requirement for state administrative reform as a condition to receiving revenue-sharing money. Although it seems unlikely that Congress, in reviewing the present general revenue-sharing legislation, will give serious consideration to stipulations requiring administrative reform, it does appear likely that pressures for placing some restrictions on the expenditure of general revenue-sharing funds will be felt. As in every legislative situation, whether or not Congress will be influenced by these demands is largely a function of the degree of pressure brought to bear by countervailing forces—in this case, urban and state ''public interest groups'' opposed to the placing of restrictions on general revenue-sharing funds. The most important of these organizations, and their tactics, are reviewed in Chapter 3.

Perhaps the most persistent and effective advocates of revenue sharing during the decades of the 1950s and 1960s were those associated with the academic community. For many of these, the advocacy of revenue sharing in particular and decentralization in general, represented a marked and abrupt departure from the main stream of political philosophy of this era—one which stressed the merits of a strong, central national government, and especially a strong and vital executive. Among these academicians, Walter Heller—at the time of his original proposal an economist at the University of Minnesota—undoubtedly was the most influential. At least one publication has bestowed upon Heller the title of "father of revenue sharing."[28] Because his thesis has been so influential and because of its impact on the legislation eventually passed, it is essential to review the outlines of the Heller proposal.

In his book, *New Dimensions of Political Economy*,[29] Heller detailed his plan that called for the setting aside each year of from 1 to 2 percent of federal income tax for distribution to the states. The money so collected would be placed in a trust fund for periodic distribution. According to Heller, the establishment of a trust fund would "underscore the fact that the states receive the funds as a matter of right" and the removal of the funds from the regular budgetary process in this manner would insure that the "revenue-sharing program would be less likely to encroach on the flow of grants-in-aid."[30] According to Heller's plan, the states would share the funds on the basis of population and states would be given "nearly complete freedom" in the use of the money. He argued that a per capita distribution of the money, rather than allocations on the basis of origin of tax collection, would insure a dispersion of the money more on the basis of need; and he proposed only that the states be required to meet the usual public auditing, accounting, and reporting requirements for public funds and that all provisions relating to nondiscriminatory use of public funds be met. Heller did suggest that the amount received by those states using the money to lower their own fiscal efforts be reduced. He also indicated that the restriction of the use of the funds to education, welfare, and community development programs might be advisable; however, he concluded that "such limitatioms are undesirable since the purpose of revenue sharing is to enlarge the states' area of fiscal discretion."[31]

The most important accomplishment of revenue sharing, argued Heller, would be the revitalization of the states. Such funds would not simply make states "better 'service stations' of federalism but (would) increase their creative and innovative energies; not simply to pay lip service to 'states' rights' but to give substance to local self-government."[32] Revenue sharing, he argued, would supply the "missing link" in the federal system by providing a dependable flow of federal funds in a form that would enlarge the options of state and local decision makers. In the final analysis, Heller believed that revenue sharing "would offer relief from the intense fiscal pressures that lead to default and dependence; would help the nation tap not only the skills and knowledge but the wisdom and ingenuity of our state and local units; and would enable these units to flex their muscles and exercise greater discretion and responsibility."[33] Revenue sharing would, he predicted, help state and local governments "hold their heads high and fulfill their intended role as strong and resilient partners in our federalism."[34]

In a 1968 publication, Heller revised his plan somewhat to allow for pass-through provisions, by which revenue-sharing money would bypass the states and be provided directly to local units of governments.[35] In making this suggestion, Heller stated that revenue sharing would "miss its mark" if it failed to relieve the fiscal pressures facing American cities. He also acknowledged that in making this suggestion he was torn between two conflicting considerations: "On the one hand, one fears—with good reason—that some states, left to their own devices, will be unwilling to share and share alike with their local units. On the other, one is reluctant to weigh the revenue-sharing plan with so many complexities that it falls of its own weight."[36] After considering the important pros and cons of each argument, Heller finally concluded that some minimum percentage pass-through amount would be desirable.

The "Heller Plan," as it became known, was immensely influential in subsequent revenue-sharing developments. The importance of this plan is reflected in the degree to which the program as finally approved in 1972 incorporates its principal ideas. The 1972 act does account for population and taxing effort in the distribution of revenue-sharing funds, does grant states (and their localities) almost total freedom in the expenditure of those funds, and does, of course, provide for direct allocation of revenue-sharing funds to the cities—bypassing state governments. However significant these parallels, Heller has been critical of some aspects of former President Nixon's "New Federalism" policy. These criticisms, among others, are discussed in Chapter 3.

It was not until 1964, at the end of Heller's term as Chairman of the Council of Economic Advisers, that his proposal began receiving serious presidential consideration. Early in 1964, federal income taxes were cut by about 20 percent because of the Administration's fear of this fiscal drag. It was also expected, at that time, that future tax cuts would be possible in the next few years. Heller's plan, then, was seen as an alternative to future tax reductions.[37]

Accordingly, in 1964, President Johnson appointed a task force headed by Joseph A. Pechman, Director of Economics at the Brookings Institution, to study the feasibility of revenue sharing. A report was made by this task force and submitted to the president; however, its details were never published. Nevertheless, it is known that Pechman favored some sort of revenue-sharing plan and that the report of the task force reflected this view. In a presentation before the American Bankers Association in 1965, Pechman stated his belief that "the fiscal pressure on the state and local governments shows no sign of easing," and that the "states will be unable to meet their growing needs without substantial additional assistance from the Federal Government."[38] The essentials of the revenue-sharing plan proposed by the Pechman task force are believed to have included the creation of a special trust fund in which approximately 2 percent of federal income tax collections would be deposited. The states would have shared in this fund in proportion to their population, and a smaller proportion of the fund would have been allocated specifically to less wealthy states. The distribution would have been annually or quarterly and the recipient units of government would have been free to use the money for general government purposes.[39] The similarities of this proposal to the Heller plan, and also to the program adopted in 1972, are obvious.

Despite the recommendations of the Pechman committee, President Johnson never acted on the revenue-sharing measure. The country's increasing involvement in the Vietnam conflict eliminated the anticipated budgetary surpluses. According to one of President Johnson's aides, "By the time they [the Pechman task force] finished the report, the Vietnam war was already draining off the surplus and labor was opposed to it."[40]

In addition to Heller and Pechman, other intellectuals were becoming critical of the "centrist-oriented" political and social philosophy that seemed to dominate government programs in the 1960s. Many of these did not offer specific proposals comparable with those of Heller's, but combined, they helped create an intellectual basis for the decentralist rationale. Some of the most important of these authors and their works include: Peter F. Drucker's *Age of Discontinuity* (Harper and Row, 1968); Daniel Moynihan's *Maximum Feasible Misunderstanding* (Free Press, 1969); James Sundquist and David Davis' *Making Federalism Work* (Brookings, 1969); and Edward Banfield's *The Unheavenly City* (Little, Brown and Company, 1970).[41]

An important essay reflecting this anti-centrist mood was published in 1966 by Richard Goodwin, former special assistant to Presidents Kennedy and Johnson.[42] In that article, entitled "The Shape of American Politics," Goodwin notes the increasing growth of centralized power in the United States. This increasing centralization and the accompanying loss of the influence of local governments and private associations has produced two major social changes, he asserts. The first "is the enormous resistance and complexity of many modern problems . . . The second is a loss of community: the fraying of human, civic, and territorial bonds between the individual and the disembodied structures which surround him."[43] As a result, he believes, the individual loses confidence in the capacity of local structures to effectively modify the political conditions of existence. In consequence, two equally undesirable reactions occur. One involves violent protests and rage; the other is manifest in the desire to protect and conserve—to seek order and security.

The way to correct this situation, Goodwin argues, is through decentralization—"by assisting and compelling states, communities, and private groups to assume a greater share of responsibility for collective action. In other words, both burden and enterprise must be shifted into units of action small enough to allow for more intimate personal contact and numerous enough to widen the outlets for direct participation and control."[44] Goodwin predicted in his essay that "the first party to carry this [decentralization] banner . . . will find itself on the right side of the decisive issues of the 1970s."[45] Although Goodwin provides an intellectual basis for decentralization, it is interesting to note that he refused, in this article, to unhesitantly endorse the revenue-sharing proposal of Walter Heller. Instead, Goodwin indicated that some program combining Heller's proposal with direct grants to cities, and with provisions that the funds be used for specific programs such as health, education, and housing would be more appropriate.

Another important intellectual critic of centralized government during this period was Peter F. Drucker. In his 1968 book, *The Age of Discontinuity*,[46] Drucker decries what he calls the "sickness" of big government. The best we get from centralized government, he believes, "is competent mediocrity. More often we do not even get that . . . In every country there are big areas of government administration where there is no performance whatever—only costs."[47] The solution, he argues, is decentralization. In his words, "'Decentralization' applied to government would not be just another form of 'federalism' in which local rather than central government discharges the 'doing' tasks. It would rather be a systematic policy of using the other, the nongovernmental institutions of the society of organizations, for the actual 'doing,' i.e., for performance, operations, execution."[48]

Thus, a considerable amount of intellectual and academic acceptance of the decentralist philosophy and of revenue sharing developed in the 1960s. It is safe to say that this philosophy was continually at odds with prevailing political and social thought of the period, but it is also certain that these "mavericks," in helping to create an intellectually acceptable climate for decentralization, had a profound impact on the revenue-sharing legislation as adopted in 1972.

President Nixon and Revenue Sharing

By the time Richard M. Nixon had gained the Republican Party's nomination for president of the United States in 1968, revenue sharing had gained considerable political, intellectual, and public support. A Gallup poll taken the preceding year had found that an overwhleming proportion of the American public supported the revenue-sharing concept. When asked to respond to the questionnaire item—"It has been suggested that 3 percent of the money which Washington collects in federal income taxes be returned to the states and local governments to be used by these states and local governments as they see fit. Do you favor or oppose this idea?"—70 percent of the American public expressed approval. There were no major differences among the various demographic groups in their support of revenue sharing as reported in the Gallop survey; however, it is interesting to note that Republicans were slightly more likely to approve of the concept than were Democrats (72 percent to 69 percent).[49]

The Republican Party platform in 1968 firmly endorsed the revenue-sharing concept. That platform pledged full federal cooperation with the efforts to revitalize state and local governments, "including revision of the system of providing federal funds and re-establishment of the authority of state governments in coordinating and administering the federal programs." The platform went on to propose "the sharing of federal revenues with state governments. We are particularly determined to revise the grant-in-aid system and substitute bloc grants wherever possible . . ."[50]

The statement by the Republican Coordinating Committee of that year went on to say that "when citizens are aggrieved by an act of government, they can generally unseat their locally elected officials . . . But they are frequently helpless and frustrated when it comes to the acts of federal agencies in Washington . . . Instead of grants for hundreds of different programs and thousands of projects, federal funds to state and local governments should be allocated to a few broad functional areas such as education, welfare, and health, with the decision as to the exact application of the funds left to the recipient governments."[51]

At the direction of President-elect Nixon, a task force on intergovernmental relations was appointed to be headed by Richard Nathan.[52] The committee's report, issued on November 29, 1968, provided a rationale for revenue sharing by stating:

Revenue sharing is an important national policy innovation for two reasons: (1) as a *fiscal tool* for dealing with the fundamental imbalance between needs and resources among the various levels of government, and (2) as a *political instrument* for decentralizing the intergovernmental fiscal policies of the federal government and giving greater decision-making authority to elected executives at the state and local levels.[53]

Arthur Burns, then Nixon's chief economic adviser, appointed an administrative task force on revenue sharing in 1969, headed by Murray L. Weidenbaum. The task force decided that the Heller-Pechman approach, with an adjustment to provide for pass-through funds, was the best proposal. In August 1969, President Nixon sent to Congress his revenue-sharing bill, which was introduced and sponsored by Senator Howard Baker. The bill, signed into law in October 1972, became the key element of the president's broader "New Federalism" package.

Alternatives to General Revenue Sharing

Revenue sharing is not without its critics, as indicated by the three-year lag between its introduction in August 1969 and its final passage in October 1972. Chapter 3 examines the specific criticisms made by the opponents of Nixon's revenue-sharing proposals. Here, it is appropriate to briefly review some of the major alternatives to the revenue-sharing concept for the sharing of national resources with state and local governments. Of course, as with revenue sharing, the validity and desirability of any of these proposals rests on the assumption that state and local governments need additional funding sources. This assumption is being questioned by some contemporary observers of federal fiscal relations.[54]

One of the most often discussed alternative methods of providing funds to state governments is that known as the *tax credit plan*. Probably the most widely cited such plan is that proposed by the Advisory Commission on Intergovernmental Relations in 1966.[55] This proposal would allow a taxpayer a federal income tax credit against increased federal tax liabilities that amounted to 40 percent of the income tax he paid to the state. As explained by Richard Nathan,[56] if, in response to the tax credit incentive, a state without an income tax did levy a new income tax that cost an individual $100, the taxpayer would actually pay only an extra $60, since $40 would be subtracted from his federal income tax liability. An individual's federal income tax liability, which would have been $1,000, would be reduced to $960. His total income tax bill would be $1060 ($960 to the federal government, $100 to his state). Thus, he would pay only $60 more in taxes, while his state would be "better off" by $100. It is argued that the plan would encourage states that do not have income taxes to adopt them and that it would substitute a progressive tax for less progressive sales and property taxes.[57] Probably the two major disadvantages of the tax credit plan are that it fails to provide for equalization of income among state governments and, of course, that about one-third of the states have not enacted income tax laws.[58]

A second alternative to revenue sharing as a means of providing fiscal assistance to states and localities is the *block grant* concept. Block grants, as defined by Michael Reagan, are "broader in scope (than categorical grants) and although tied to a clearly stated area (such as health or elementary education, or community facilities development) they do not specify the exact objectives of permitted expenditures and hence create much larger zones of discretion on the part of the receiving government . . ."[59] Examples of block grant programs would include the Partnership in Health Act of 1966 and the 1966 Model Cities program. The Nixon special revenue-sharing proposals (in the areas of law enforcement, community development, transportation, rural development, education, and manpower) are similar to block grants in that the money would be allocated to specific functions.[60] Probably the major criticism of the block grant approach is that it would divorce the responsibility for collecting taxes from decisions on their use—that is, some would argue that the level of government raising money has the major obligation for determining how that money is to be spent, and it is argued that block grants fail to follow this principle.

The third major alternative to revenue sharing would simply be a continuation of the *categorical grant* approach, which has dominated the system of grants-in-aid since the Civil War. By 1972, as previously discussed, it was estimated that the number of such programs was approaching 600.[61] Nathan has identified four major groupings of such programs that include: "narrowly defined formula-type grants" (such as the National Defense Education Act); "highway and public assistance grants;" "broadly defined formula-type grants" (such as Title I of the Elementary and Secondary Education Act, 1965); and "project aid" (urban renewal).[62] As mentioned above, the distinguishing characteristics of categorical grants are that they are allocated to specific and narrowly defined purposes and that they generally include a considerable amount of federal supervision and oversight. It is this federal supervision and control that supporters of revenue sharing have most deplored.

Much of this chapter has reviewed the arguments favoring revenue sharing and the decentralization of decision-making. It is also important to note that philosophical justifications for the continuation of a certain degree of federal supervision have been advanced as well. Chapter 3 explores in greater detail the various political and social consequences of decentralization. It is only important to point out here that the thesis of scholars such as E.E. Schattschneider,[63] who have argued persuasively that the broader the scope of decision making, the more likely are decisions to satisfy the "public interest" and the less likely are the interests of minority segments of the population to be ignored. Perhaps the greatest threat of revenue sharing (and thus the major justification for a continuation of the categorical or block grant system) is that it narrows the locus of decision making to a level that may be unsympathetic and unattentive to minority interests. According to one observer, revenue sharing "is a cop-out rather than a panacea as far as the responsibilities of the national government to make real judgments of its own in response to its own analysis of domestic needs is concerned."[64]

There are, then, various alternatives to revenue sharing as a means of providing fiscal assistance to state and local governments. Like revenue sharing, each of these has its advantages and disadvantages, and it is clear that the support of one program over the other is as much a *political* as a *fiscal* decision. Some groups tend to benefit from one alternative while others benefit from another. This, of course, explains the enormous public interest in revenue sharing and the potential importance of general revenue sharing for federalism. The degree to which certain groups and functions are advantaged by general revenue sharing—to the extent that this can be measured with existing data—is examined in depth in Chapters 4 and 5.

Conclusion

This chapter has reviewed the historical development of general revenue sharing. It is clear that general revenue sharing is not an entirely new concept and that some would trace its beginnings to the pre-Civil War period—prior, even, to the development of the categorical grant system of the intergovernmental aid. However, the concept was "rediscovered" in the 1950s and 1960s, and new philosophic and fiscal justifications were offered in its defense.

Concerning fiscal affairs, it appeared to many that state and local governments were facing an impending financial crisis. The debts of these units of government were rapidly increasing, their employment roles were rapidly expanding, demands for their services were increasing, and their ability to raise revenue was largely curtailed. On the other hand, the national government, with its heavy reliance on income tax revenue, was at a fiscal advantage. The solution, for many, was a sharing of federal revenues.

Philosophically, general revenue sharing and the entire decentralization concept gained academic and intellectual acceptance in this period. Much of the political and social thought of these years advocated a strong centralized government and especially defended the need for a strong chief executive. However, there were those who were beginning to question this "centrist" doctrine. For these "defectors," big government often resulted in alienation and anomie, and they viewed decentralization as a means of reversing these trends.

Above all, it must be stressed that general revenue sharing and the impact it may have on federal relations has its political as well as its fiscal and philosophic implications. Political scientists have long realized that federalism, and its changing nature, are more than simply legal and constitutional arrangements of governmental units. Rather, the changing nature of federalism affects not only the *locus* of decision making, but more importantly, it may affect the *content* of decisions as well. General revenue sharing may mean more than simply a shift in decision-making power from Washington to America's mayors and governors (although if it happens, that in itself is significant), it may alter the decisions themselves. Thus, when examining general revenue sharing, it becomes important to ask, "Who benefits and who loses?" In general, the theory of federalism would argue that as the scope of decision making is enlarged, decisions that are redistributive and in the interest of the politically disadvantaged are more likely to be reached. As the locus of decision making is decreased, it is argued that decisions that are conservative and status-quo-oriented are more likely to be reached.[65] It would be expected, then, that general revenue sharing with its emphasis on decentralization of decision making would result in more conservative urban public policy. However, it might be true, as Suzanne Farkas has pointed out[66] that these conventional assumptions of federalism may be more appropriate to theory and to history than to contemporary urban politics. The categorical grant programs of the 1960s, even if they failed to eradicate poverty and slums, did succeed in politicizing large numbers of otherwise apathetic and politically naive inner city residents. These groups have become a potent and decisive force in the politics of many urban areas. As decision making is decentralized, it is possible that these organizatione may use their influence to veto reactive urban policies or even to promote socially-oriented, redistributive programs. To the extent that these effects can be documented, a reassessment of the political effects of federalism clearly would be in order. These concerns are pursued in the following chapters.

Notes

1. Robert L. Heilbroner, "The Share-the-Tax-Revenue Plan," *New York Times Sunday Magazine*, December 27, 1964, p. 8.

2. Thomas R. Dye, *Politics in States and Communities* (Englewood Cliffs, N.J.: Prentice-Hall, 1973), p. 536.

3. An informative account of this act and its provisions may be found in Maureen McBreen, "Federal Tax Sharing: Historical Development and

Arguments for and against Recent Proposals," in *Revenue Sharing and Its Alternatives*, prepared for the Subcommittee on Fiscal Policy, Joint Economic Committee, U.S., Congress, 90th Cong., 1st Sess. (Washington, D.C.: Government Printing Office, 1967), pp. 717-8.

4. Ibid., p. 718.

5. Ibid.

6. Jane P. Clark, *The Rise of a New Federalism* (New York: Russell and Russell, 1965), p. 140.

7. Ibid.

8. For example, see Richard P. Nathan, "The Policy Setting: Analysis of Major Post-Vietnam Federal Aid Policy Alternatives," in *Revenue Sharing and Its Alternatives*, pp. 666-84.

9. See Clark, *The Rise of a New Federalism*, p. 142.

10. The 1969 *Catalog of Federal Domestic Assistance* (Office of Economic Opportunity, Washington, D.C.: Government Printing Office, 1969), lists 581 such programs.

11. Reported in *National Journal*, April 3, 1971, p. 710.

12. Michael D. Reagan, *The New Federalism* (New York; Oxford University Press, 1972), p. 90.

13. U.S. Bureau of the Census, *Government Finances in 1968-69* (Washington, D.C.: Government Printing Office, 1970).

14. For an excellent discussion of this fiscal imbalance, see Advisory Commission on Intergovernmental Relations, *Revenue Sharing–An Idea Whose Time Has Come* (Washington, D.C.: Government Printing Office, 1970).

15. Ibid., pp. 4-5.

16. Henry S. Reuss, *Revenue-Sharing: Crutch or Catalyst for State and Local Governments?* (New York: Praeger, 1970), p. 6.

17. Actually, many now argue that the concern of this period with municipal bankruptcy and chronic state budgetary deficits was largely exaggerated. As noted in the recent Brookings Institution study on national priorities, the "fiscal crisis" of state and local governments "began to abate as the economy began to pick up in 1972 and that fiscal projections for the next decade do not anticipate a long-run imbalance similar to the 1970 to 1972 period." See Edward R. Fried, Alice M. Rivlin, Charles L. Schultze, and Nancy J. Teeters, *Setting National Priorities: The 1974 Budget* (Washington, D.C.: The Brookings Institution, 1973), p. 269.

18. Reported in Dom Bonafede, "Revenue-Sharing Report/The Nixon Plan's Premise: America's Federal System is Not Working," *National Journal*, April 3, 1971, p. 711.

19. Excerpts from speech of Hon. Melvin R. Laird of Wisconsin, in U.S., Congress, House of Representatives, February 15, March 13, and April 10, 1967, found in *Revenue Sharing and Its Alternatives*, p. 890-913.

20. Ibid., p. 911.

21. See McBreen, "Federal Tax Sharing," in *Revenue Sharing and Its Alternatives*, p. 721.

22. Republican Coordinating Committee, *Financing the Future of Federalism: The Case for Revenue Sharing*, Task Force on the Functions of Federal, State and Local Government, Washington, D.C.; March, 1966.

23. Research paper issued jointly by the Republican Governors' Association and the Ripon Society, July, 1965. This paper may be found in *Revenue Sharing and Its Alternatives*, p. 962-71.

24. As quoted in McBreen, "Federal Tax Sharing," in *Revenue Sharing and Its Alternatives*, p. 716.

25. Reuss, *Revenue Sharing*, p. 124.

26. Ibid., pp. 125-26.

27. Ibid., p. 142.

28. *National Journal*, April 3, 1971, p. 710.

29. Walter W. Heller, *New Dimensions of Political Economy* (Cambridge, Mass.: Harvard University Press, 1966).

30. Ibid., p. 146.

31. Ibid., p. 147.

32. Ibid., p. 168.

33. Ibid., p. 169.

34. Ibid.

35. Walter W. Heller, "A Sympathetic Reappraisal of Revenue Sharing," in Harvey S. Perloff and Richard P. Nathan (eds.), *Revenue Sharing and the City* (Baltimore: John Hopkins Press, 1968), pp. 3-39.

36. Ibid., p. 31.

37. A concise history of these events may be found in L.L. Ecker-Racz, *The Politics and Economics of State-Local Finance* (Englewood Cliffs, N.J.: Prentice-Hall, 1970), pp. 186-7.

38. Joseph A. Pechman, "Financing State and Local Governments," from Proceedings of a Symposium on Federal Taxation sponsored by The American Bankers Association, Friday, March 26, 1965, Washington, D.C. This paper may be found in *Revenue Sharing and Its Alternatives*, pp. 763-74.

39. A discussion of these may be found in Ecker-Racz, *The Politics and Economics of State-Local Finance*, p. 187.

40. As quoted in the *National Journal*, April 3, 1971, p. 711.

41. A brief review of these works may be found in: *National Journal*, December 16, 1972, p. 1919.

42. Richard N. Goodwin, "The Shape of American Politics," *Commentary* (June 1967), pp. 25-40.

43. Ibid., p. 29.

44. Ibid., p. 36.

45. Ibid.

46. Peter F. Drucker, *The Age of Discontinuity* (New York: Harper and Row, 1968).

47. Ibid., p. 218.

48. Ibid., p. 234.

49. *Gallop Poll*, January 1, 1967.

50. Excerpts of the 1968 Republican Party Platform may be found in *National Journal*, April 3, 1971, p. 721.

51. Excerpts of this report may be found in ibid., p. 711.

52. The following discussion relies heavily on the report to be found in the *National Journal*, April 3, 1971, p. 712.

53. Ibid.

54. As discussed in above, see footnote 17. Many economists predicted more favorable economic conditions for local government in the foreseeable future.

55. Advisory Commission on Intergovernmental Relations, *Federal-State Coordination of Personal Income Taxes* (Washington, D.C.: Government Printing Office, 1966).

56. Nathan, "The Policy Setting: Analysis of Major Post-Vietnam Federal Aid Policy Alternatives," p. 678-9.

57. Werner Z. Hirsch, *The Economics of State and Local Government* (New York: McGraw-Hill, 1970), p. 126.

58. See Heller, *New Dimensions of Political Economy*, pp. 157-8; and Reuss, *Revenue Sharing,* pp. 114-5 for criticisms of the tax credit plan.

59. Reagan, *New Federalism*, p. 59.

60. President Nixon's special revenue-sharing proposals differed from the block grant concept primarily in that they would eliminate existing requirements for matching funds.

61. See 1969 *Catalog of Federal Domestic Assistance*.

62. Nathan, "The Policy Setting: Analysis of Major Post-Vietnam Federal Aid Policy Alternatives," p. 672.

63. E.E. Schattschneider, *The Semi-Sovereign People* (New York: Holt, Rinehart and Winston, 1960).

64. Reagan, *New Federalism*, pp. 130-1.

65. Schattschneider, *The Semi-Sovereign People*, p. 9.

66. Suzanne Farkas, "The Federal Role in Urban Decentralization," in Richard D. Feld and Carl Crafton (eds.), *The Uneasy Partnership* (Palo Alto, Cal.: National Press Books, 1973), p. 162.

The State and Local Fiscal Assistance Act of 1972

Introduction

As finally passed in October 1972, general revenue sharing is to return over $30 billion to state and local governments during its five-year life. In terms of financial outlays alone, the program rivals the man-on-the-moon project of the 1960s. However, to former President Nixon, general revenue sharing was far more important than its fiscal outlay would indicate. For the Nixon Administration, general revenue sharing was to have been the cornerstone of a much larger program labeled by the Administration as the "New Federalism"; and new federalism, according to the president, was paramount to a new American revolution.[1] For its supporters, the "New Federalism" philosophy promised to alleviate the fiscal crisis of state and local governments,[2] to make local governments more responsive to local needs, and to reverse the centralizing tendencies in the American system. To others, the program appeared to be simply an abandonment by the federal government of its long standing commitment to a variety of socially oriented programs and an abdication of many of its responsibilities in the areas of human rights and welfare. This chapter examines in depth the revenue-sharing act as passed in 1972, discusses the forces helping to shape the outcome of the bill, and explores the outlines of the "New Federalism" philosophy and the role of general revenue sharing in that philosophy.

President Nixon's Commitment to General Revenue Sharing

The reasons for Richard Nixon's strong commitment to revenue sharing are somewhat obscure. As mentioned in Chapter 2, following its long history, the revenue-sharing concept was finally endorsed in 1968 by the Republican Coordinating Committee and became a key plank in the Republican platform of that year. In one sense, then, President Nixon, in his attachment to the plan, was only carrying out the wishes of his party as expressed in the platform and the 1968 campaign. Obviously, however, Nixon's firm commitment to revenue sharing (almost three years of intensive legislative struggle were required for its passage) went far beyond whatever ceremonial obligations any president may feel toward his party's platform. President Nixon's dedication to revenue sharing, a plan designed specifically to assist state and local governments, is even more interesting given the fact that he never held a nonfederal elective office. Even those serving in the Nixon Administration offered differing explanations for his support of revenue sharing.[3]

For some, Nixon's motives were basically intellectual and philosophical. According to Richard Thompson's account, President Nixon was especially disturbed by the maze of federal programs that had developed since the New Deal.[4] The effect of these programs, Nixon believed, was to centralize power in Washington, and he seemed convinced that centralization created more social ills than it solved. Repeating a theme similar to that advocated by the "decentralist" academicians and intellectuals reviewed in Chapter 2, President Nixon expressed in his public speeches a concern with the debilitating effects of centralized power and "big government" on individuals. "The time has now come in America," he said in his 1971 State of the Union Address, "to reverse the flow of power and resources from the states and communities to Washington, and start power and resources flowing back . . . to the states and communities and, more important, to the people all across America." In that speech, President Nixon also stated his belief that "The further away government is from people, the stronger government becomes and the weaker people become . . . Let's face it, most Americans today are simply fed up with government . . . As everything seems to have grown bigger and more complex in America, as the forces that shape our lives seem to have grown more distant and more impersonal, a great feeling of frustration has crept across this land."[5] Commenting on President Nixon's philosophy, one of his aides stated, "You may laugh at me for this, but I think the President is an intellectual. And this is an intellectual decision he has made—that government can be made more responsive to the people only by bringing government closer to the people."[6]

Of course, pragmatic political reasons for President Nixon's endorsement can also be cited. On the one hand, it is sometimes argued that general revenue sharing in particular and new federalism in general, with its elimination of many categorical grant programs, may result in a loss of power by Congress but a new gain in power and influence by the presidency as well as by states and localities. Speaking before a meeting of mayors in December 1973, Representative Thomas L. Ashley of Ohio stated that new federalism, as put into practice by the Nixon Administration, has meant "aggrandizement of power in the White House at the expense of Congress."[7] Thus, some feel that general revenue sharing, in part at least, was a calculated attempt by the Administration to usurp congressional authority.

At the same time, it is sometimes suggested that revenue sharing was a politically convenient tactic in the election year of 1972, by which President Nixon could gain the support of governors and big city mayors and thus neutralize or reduce the opposition of key elements of the traditional Democratic coalition. According to Thompson, "Nixon wooed Democratic mayors and governors who might be tempted to criticize his stewardship of domestic affairs. He gained an unexpected political byproduct when Democratic congressmen and senators who opposed revenue sharing found themselves in serious disagreement with Democratic mayors and governors who supported it.[8]

Whatever his motives, whether out of a concern for his obligation to his party's platform, for philosophical reasons, or for political gain, Nixon closely allied himself with general revenue sharing, and the measure became the central element in his domestic policy. Despite this strong position, it is clear that congressional opposition to the measure was strong, and an intensive effort on the part of the president and groups interested in its passage was necessary for its adoption.

The Legislative Process: 1969-1972

On August 13, 1969, President Nixon sent to Congress his first general revenue-sharing proposal. This plan, introduced in the Senate by Howard Baker and in the House by Jackson Betts, was for a much smaller sum of shared revenues than the measure eventually adopted. Nixon's 1969 proposal called for an initial sharing of $500 million, to be increased to $5 billion by 1976. In his 1969 revenue-sharing measure, he also proposed that a certain proportion of the money returned to each state be automatically made available to local governments in each state. According to the bill's formula, approximately 30 percent of each state's funds would have been passed on to the localities.[9] No hearings were held on the president's proposal, although the Senate Government Operations Subcommittee on Intergovernmental Relations did conduct hearings concerning a revenue-sharing bill sponsored by Senators Muskie and Goodell.[10]

In the following months, intensive efforts by members of the Administration, state and local organizations, and various "public interest" groups to persuade Congress to act on the measure were initiated. In the Spring of 1970, more than 2,000 state and local officials attended a Washington conference at which they voiced their support of general revenue sharing. In April 1970, heads of the major state and local government organizations,[11] held a joint press conference urging Congress (and especially Wilbur Mills, Chairman of the House Ways and Means Committee and Russell Long, Chairman of the Senate Finance Committee) to hold hearings on the general revenue-sharing measure.[12] In meetings with governors of the Appalachian states and Northern Plains states in July 1970, President Nixon reiterated his support of general revenue sharing.[13] During the fall congressional campaign, members of several state and local government organizations contacted every member of Congress running for re-election to seek their support for general revenue sharing. By the end of 1970, almost 200 Representatives and 59 Senators indicated that they would support the basic principles of revenue sharing.[14] By the end of 1970, it was clear that the Nixon Administration had made a major commitment to general revenue sharing. According to one account, this decision largely explains a string of presidential vetoes in late 1970 in the areas of health, education, welfare, and manpower measures. The president did not wish to extend or create new categorical grant programs at a time when the administration was formulating its major commitment to the general revenue-sharing concept.[15] After the 1970 election, President Nixon decided to expand general revenue sharing both in concept and funding level.

President Nixon's 1971 State of the Union Address probably stands as his most eloquent and detailed defense of general revenue sharing and, indeed, of the "New Federalism" concept. One of "six great goals" that he offered to Congress in that speech was designed to "strengthen and to renew our State and local governments." Since the founding of the nation, the president told Congress, power has been flowing toward the central government. The time has come, he said, to reverse this flow of power and to develop "a new partnership between the Federal Government and the States and localities—a partnership in which we entrust the States and localities with a larger share of the Nation's responsibilities, and in which we share our Federal revenues with them so that they can meet those responsibilities. To achieve this goal, I propose . . . that we enact a plan of revenue sharing historic in scope and bold in concept."[16]

The plan, as President Nixon outlined in his State of the Union Address, would make a $16 billion "investment" in state and local governments. Five billion dollars would have been allocated to a general revenue-sharing program from which the funds would be used as states and localities saw fit, the other $11 billion would have been provided primarily by consolidating various categorical grant programs into a series of "special" revenue-sharing measures. His plan, Nixon believed, would realign state and federal priorities and responsibilities. The federal role would still be important in achieving national goals, but states and localities would have a much greater role than in the past. Established functions and new programs, which clearly were federal in nature, still would be performed by the national government; where state and local governments could do better jobs, the purpose was to provide them with the financial resources to do so. President Nixon concluded by stating:

Under this plan, the Federal Government will provide the States and localities with more money and less interference—and by cutting down the interference the same amount of money will go a lot further.[17]

Nixon's "revised" general revenue-sharing bill then was introduced to Congress on February 9, 1971, again sponsored by Senator Howard Baker. The plan would have made available to the states and localities a sum equal to 1.3 percent of federal taxable income (or approximately $5 billion in 1971). Under this proposal, 90 percent of the available funds would have been allocated to the states according to their populations, with adjustments made for taxing efforts. The remaining 10 percent would have been allocated to those states negotiating a formula for sharing federal funds with local governments.[18]

Of the total share allotted to each state under the Nixon plan, approximately 50 percent would have been passed on to local governments (excluding school districts and other special purpose governments). The amount distributed to each locality would have been based on the local government's taxing effort. If a city raised 10 percent of all local revenue in its state, it would receive 10 percent of the pass-through revenue-sharing funds. States would not have been bound to this pass-through formula, and, as mentioned above, a 10 percent incentive payment would be available to states negotiating different formulae with their local governments. The only provision attached to the Nixon proposal was that governors would have to pledge to use the money only for government purposes and the Secretary of the Treasury was authorized to refer any noncompliance with federal antidiscrimination laws to the Attorney General.[19]

General Revenue Sharing and the House of Representatives

In the House of Representatives debates on general revenue sharing, two influential House leaders—Wilbur Mills, Chairman of the Ways and Means Committee, and George Mahon, Chairman of the Appropriations Committee—were opposed to each other.[20] Mills' position is particularly interesting. On January 25, 1971 (14 days before the Nixon proposal was officially introduced), Mills publicly stated that "I am perfectly willing to have hearings [on revenue sharing], but not for the purpose of promoting the plan—for the purpose of killing it."[21] When House hearings on the bill began (June 2, 1971), Mills' opposition appeared adamant. Following Treasury Secretary John Connally's presentation of the merits of general revenue sharing before the House Ways and Means Committee, the following exchange between Mills and Connally took place:

CHAIRMAN MILLS: Mr. Secretary, we thank you for your statement. I want to congratulate you on making a very fine statement in behalf of a very weak cause.

MR. CONNALLY: I understand, Mr. Chairman, that is not your favorite subject.

CHAIRMAN MILLS: No sir, it is not. . . . I have great fear that this program would operate just the opposite of all the platitudes and verbiage you use here in describing it. . . . I think, frankly, the only way I can describe this proposal is that you brought a Trojan Horse into the committee room . . . I think this is the most dangerous proposal that has ever been developed, and I say that in all sincerity.[22]

Reportedly, Chairman Mills based his objections on four critical points.

1. The Administration's general revenue-sharing proposal would have distributed funds to local governments without adequately accounting for need.

2. The "no strings attached" provision of the Nixon Administration's proposal would divorce the responsibility for raising revenue from the spending of revenue.

3. Revenue sharing would add another "uncontrollable expenditure" to the federal budget.

4. Revenue sharing would not encourage state and local governments to help themselves.[23]

Despite his strong early statements, Mills, midway through the hearings, switched his position, and by late summer of 1971, he stated: "I personally would not be opposed to providing federal grants to local governments to aid those cities and communities which face truly acute, immediate problems and which can prove their needs."[24] Mills' switch seemed prompted, in part at least, by an intensive lobbying effort conducted by such state and locally oriented organizations as the National League of Cities and the U.S. Conference of Mayors.[25]

Congressman Mahon's objections were more unswerving than Mills'. Mahon objected to the bill on two grounds: (1) it spent money he did not believe the government had; and (2) it appropriated funds in a legislative bill.[26] Ordinarily, a program is established in one bill and funds for the activity are appropriated in a separate bill initiated by the Appropriations Committee, chaired by Mahon. Placing the bill under the supervision of the Appropriations Committee probably would have meant that state and local governments would have received their funds only after an annual justification of their needs to the Appropriations Committee. President Nixon's domestic advisor, John Ehrlichman, commented that treating general revenue sharing as a regular appropriations bill probably would not have killed the measure but, he said, "it is antithetical to the whole concept of general revenue sharing to put it under appropriations."[27] Even after the passage of general revenue sharing, Mahon continued his criticism. Revenue sharing, he said, is "manna from heaven" in the eyes of state and local government, and the pressure for expansion of the program will be irresistible, he believed. "Already the mayors are clamoring to boost it from $6 billion to $8 billion. When they get that, then they will want $10 billion, and so on.''[28]

Of course, support for and opposition to the general revenue-sharing bill were not confined to the Nixon Administration and Congress. As would be expected, the bill attracted a considerable amount of attention among various public interest groups, as well. Probably the most intense lobbying effort by a private organization *against* general revenue sharing was waged by the AFL-CIO. AFL-CIO's opposition was based on several points: it was feared that revenue sharing would threaten on-going categorical grant programs; it would be difficult or impossible to enforce federal civil rights legislation under the provisions of the act; it would make federal regulation of the economy more difficult; and state and local governments were not in a position to adequately meet national needs. Testifying before the hearings of the House Ways and Means Committee considering the bill, Andrew J. Biemiller, Director of the Department of Legislation, AFL-CIO, stated:

The AFL-CIO is firmly opposed to a concept of no-strings, no standards, and no supervision revenue sharing. There is no justification for the adoption of a new federal aid delivery system which is specifically designed to bypass the process of congressional legislation, appropriation, and oversight . . . [The problems of states and localities] can be solved largely by an improvement in the existing system and in a substantial increase in Federal grants. And, in many cases, the programs that could provide the funds are already in operation, under federal law.

No-strings revenue sharing is not the answer to the needs of cities and smaller government units. Indeed, it is a wasteful inefficient method of dispensing critically needed federal aid. [29]

Organized labor endorsed other means of assisting state and local governments and proposed especially that federal categorical grant-in-aid programs—with federal standards, federal guidelines, and federal review procedures—should be strengthened and continued. A legislative representative for the AFL-CIO stated, ''If the Administration has suddenly found $5 billion in extra money, it is our feeling they should do something with it that has higher priority than revenue sharing.''[30]

Other organizations expressed varying degrees of dissatisfaction with the general revenue-sharing concept.[31] In a 1971 position paper, the American Federation of State, County and Municipal Employees stated their opposition: ''While we do not have a closed mind on the issue of revenue sharing, we do have a serious question on a 'no strings' approach to the channeling of federal dollars back down to states and municipalities. . . Equally important, we oppose any attempt to use revenue sharing as a gambit for siphoning off appropriations from federal grant-in-aid programs as a disguised method of delivering 'new' funds to the states and cities.'' [32] Also, various civil libertarian groups, such as the American Civil Liberties Union, and those dedicated to fighting racial discrimination, were opposed to general revenue sharing. In a resolution adopted at its 1971 national convention, the National Association for the Advancement of Colored People resolved that "The NAACP calls upon the Congress to reject any revenue-sharing plan which fails to provide workable safeguards against discrimination based on geography, population and/or race in the distribution and utilization of public funds."[33]

For the most part, the opposition to general revenue sharing, outside of Congress, was relatively disorganized, sporadic, and ineffective. Compared with this was the highly organized and united effort of the various organizations of state and local governments in support of revenue sharing. These organizations included the National League of Cities, the United States Conference of Mayors, the International City Management Association, the National Association of Counties, the National Governors' Conference, the Council of State Governments, and the National Legislative Conference.[34] Although these groups are often in conflict over specific national policy, they were in agreement concerning their support of general revenue sharing. Perhaps the most active of these groups was the joint association of the National League of Cities and United States Conference of Mayors. In order to promote general revenue sharing, the organization established a Legislative Action Committee in 1970, consisting of mayors of major cities. According to Thompson, "Each month, members of the Legislative Action Committee traveled to different American cities and presented a well-publicized 'road show' for the media and community leaders. They documented the problems threatening urban America and urged support of revenue sharing. [The groups] also met privately several times with the congressional leadership—cajoling and pleading at times, and threatening at others—to convince them of the necessity of revenue sharing."[35]

Representatives of these organizations also presented their appeals before various congressional bodies. Testifying before the House Ways and Means Committee, Indianapolis Mayor Richard Lugar, speaking in support of general revenue sharing as a spokesman for the National League of Cities, stated: "We want to point out that we believe that localities in America are the best place to determine national priorities in a diverse and complex country."[36] Speaking before the same committee, Mayor E. A. Mosher of Topeka stated that ". . . general revenue sharing . . . is the most promising concept yet devised for those of us who want a balanced federal system, a system where our local, state, as well as our National Government in full partnership can cooperatively and responsibly meet the needs of the people."[37] As a final example, Cleveland Mayor Carl Stokes, in his position as First Vice President of the National League of Cities, testified before the committee that "It is on behalf of local flexibility, local determination of the proper allocation of resources, local accountability, and local responsibility that I urge your favorable consideration of general revenue sharing.''[38] Through such public and legislative presentations, these organizations presented a solid, united, and formidable lobbying effort on behalf of general revenue sharing.

In spite of the intense lobbying efforts of these organizations and in spite of Chairman Mills' unexpected support of general revenue sharing, there was little consensus among the other House Ways and Means Committee members concerning the measure and the Committee could not agree on the specifics of a bill. According to Thompson's account, on August 5, representatives of the state and local government interest groups met with Mills in an attempt to expedite the legislation. Mills directed that these representatives work with John Martin, chief counsel to the Ways and Means Committee and Lawrence Woodworth of the staff of the Joint Committee on Internal Revenue Taxation in an attempt to produce an acceptable bill. The major guidelines desired by Mills included a larger portion of the funds for local governments; distribution of the funds to localities on the basis of need; and involvement of all levels of government.[39] In a message to Congress on September 9, 1971, President Nixon repeated his strong support of general revenue sharing and urged congressional action on the measure. In that speech Nixon stated, ''I again urge the Congress to act in this session on the far-reaching proposal of revenue sharing which I have prepared to help revitalize our state and local governments and to ease the crushing rise in the burden of property taxes in this country.''[40]

On November 30, 1971, Mills and nine other members of the House Ways and Means Committee introduced a version of the revenue-sharing bill entitled, ''Intergovernmental Fiscal Coordination Act of 1971.'' However, this bill was disappointing to many state and local advocates of revenue sharing. In spite of the fact that the Mills bill contained $1 billion extra for local governments and in spite of Mills' assertion that his program would allocate funds on the basis of need, it was found that most large cities would receive less money under Mills' program than under the Nixon Administration's.[41] State and local government interest groups, including especially the National League of Cities and the U.S. Conference of Mayors, pressed for changes in Mills' formula.

Likewise, President Nixon maintained his strong support of his own revenue-sharing bill. In his 1972 State of the Union Address (delivered on January 20, 1972), President Nixon stated:

Two and one-half years ago . . . I presented a program for sharing Federal revenues with State and local governments. Last year I greatly expanded on this concept. Yet, despite undisputed evidence of compelling needs, despite overwhelming public support, despite the endorsement of both major political parties and most of the Nation's Governors and mayors, and despite the fact that most other nations with federal systems of government already have such a program, revenue sharing still remains on the list of unfinished business. I call again today for the enactment of revenue sharing.[42]

Finally, on April 26, 1972, the House Ways and Means Committee reported a "clean" version of the revenue-sharing bill, entitled the "State and Local Fiscal Assistance Act of 1972." The bill provided that two-thirds of the shared funds would go to local governments and one-third would go to the states. In justifying these proportions, the committee stated in its report:

In considering the financial problem of local governments [the] committee came to the conclusion that many localities face most severe financial crises . . . Closely related to this is the problem arising from the limited jurisdictions of many local governments: they often are called upon to provide many services for persons who do not live in their taxing jurisdictions. At the same time, those within their taxing jurisdictions often are poor and unable to pay for their share of the services demanded. [This] committee concluded that states also have financial problems but that their problems are less severe than those of the localities and also of a different nature . . . [This] committee concluded that, in the case of the states, the primary emphasis should be on encouraging them to help themselves—by making more extensive use of their own resources.[43]

As approved by the Ways and Means Committee, the bill appropriated $3.5 billion per year for local governments for five years. In addition, it appropriated funds for state governments at an initial rate of $1.8 billion and increased that rate by $150 million for the following year and by $300 million for each succeeding year.

The bill also created a complex distribution system.[44] The allocation of state funds was to be according to total tax effort and income tax collections. State tax effort was to be calculated by a formula relating the total tax collections of a state and its local governments, including special purpose units, to total personal income in the state. The state's allocation would then be determined by establishing the proportion of its tax efforts to the total U.S. state and local tax effort. Each state's share would be approximately 7.5 percent of its income taxation. For those states having no income tax, a minimum amount was guaranteed; and no state was to receive more than 3 percent of federal income tax liabilities arising from the state.

For local governments, the distribution was even more complicated. The total available was to be divided into three equal portions, to be allocated among the states on the basis of three factors: (1) total state population, (2) urban population, and (3) population weighted by per capita income. Each state's local funds were to be allocated among its counties according to these same factors. The amount going to county governments was to be determined according to the proportion of total local taxes raised in the county. The remaining funds were to be distributed to the municipal governments according to three factors: (1) the allocation based on population was to be distributed according to the relative population of the municipality; (2) funds allocated according to an inverse population per capita income ratio were to be distributed on that basis among the municipalities; and (3) funds allocated according to urban population were to be distributed in proportion to the totals distributed under the other two factors. According to this House bill, states were authorized to increase the proportion of available funds to be allocated to their localities by as much as 40 percent and to decrease the proportion by as much as 25 percent. Also, the bill denied funds to any locality if its total allocation would be less than $200 and authorized states to withhold up to 10 percent of local funds for regional projects provided the states equally matched the local funds with state funds.

In addition to fundamentally altering the distribution of revenue-sharing funds as proposed by the Nixon Administration, the bill as approved by the House Ways and Means Committee provided for more "strings" and regulations. Funds allocated to local governments were limited in use to "generally recognized . . . national high-priority objectives."[45] Also, the bill excluded the expenditure of revenue-sharing funds in such major areas as education and welfare because of existing national efforts in those areas and required states to maintain at least the level of aid to their local governments as that prevailing prior to revenue sharing.

The House, in a key procedural vote on June 21, 1972, accepted a "closed rule" provision for debating the revenue-sharing bill. This rule limited the House floor action to passing the bill, defeating the bill, or sending it back to the Ways and Means Committee. In his heated objection to this provision, Congressman Mahon stated:

Not in the history of Congress that I can find has an appropriations bill come to the floor of the House under a closed rule . . . . I say it is indefensible that the appropriations bill of $30 billion should come before the House next week under a closed rule.[46]

Despite the objections of Mahon and others, the House version was approved on June 22 by a commanding vote of 275 to 122.

General Revenue Sharing and the Senate

The Senate Committee on Finances began hearings on the bill on June 29. During these hearings, Treasury Secretary George Shultz urged the Senate to consider several changes in the House version. He suggested that the House bill placed too much emphasis on state income taxes, placed too many restrictions on the use of revenue-sharing funds, and unfairly discriminated against sparsely populated states.

The revenue-sharing bill reported by the Senate Finance Committee was substantially different from the House version. Although the Senate bill provided the same total amount of revenue sharing as did the House bill, it authorized, in addition, supplementary social service grants, reduced the proportion of funds allocated to more urbanized states, and increased the proportion allocated to urbanized areas. The Senate version also eliminated the restrictions on the use of revenue-sharing funds provided in the House bill.

In an interesting maneuver, Senate supporters of the bill—in an attempt to keep the measure out of the normal appropriations process—included in the bill a provision establishing a permanent revenue-sharing fund consisting of 7 percent of personal income tax receipts for the five-year period covered by the bill. The Secretary of the Treasury was directed to pay from the trust fund to state and local governments their share based on the formula approved. It was expected that the fund would provide more than enough to meet the financial obligations of the bill, and any remaining amount was to be turned over to the general funds of the Treasury. Such a tactic was designed to insulate the revenue-sharing program from the necessity of yearly consideration as normally required of appropriations measures.

In determining the allocation of revenue-sharing funds, the Senate version of the bill provided that each state's share would be based on its total population, total tax effort, and per capita income. Two-thirds of each state's allocation was to be passed on to local governments. The local governments' share for each state was to be determined by a formula accounting for population, tax effort, and inverse per capita income. The Senate version also established a floor and a ceiling so that no county or municipality would receive less than 20 percent or more than 145 percent of the average per capita allocation of all local governments in a state; disallowed allocation of a share to any locality entitled to less than $200; and required each recipient government to submit an annual report to the Treasury Department describing the purposes for which the funds were used.

In floor debates on the Senate bill, a number of amendments were offered such as the one by Abraham Ribicoff that would have granted larger shares of funds to the most populous and industrialized states. Ribicoff's amendment was defeated by a vote of 61 to 24. Vance Hartke offered an amendment, approved by the Senate, which was to apply existing federal labor standards to projects funded with revenue-sharing funds. In addition, an amendment offered by James Buckley to limit revenue sharing to two years was defeated. The Senate passed the bill, in its amended form, on September 12, by a vote of 64 to 20.

Final Congressional Action: The State and Local Fiscal
Assistance Act of 1972

The House and Senate conference report allowed each state to receive the larger of the allocations, applying either the House or Senate approved distribution formula. The House formula, based on five factors (population, urbanization, per capita income, income tax collections, and general tax effort), provides larger amounts to more urbanized states; the Senate formula, based on three factors (population, general tax effort, and per capita income), favors the less populous, rural states. In addition, the conference committee adopted the Senate's version of how the state's total allocation would be distributed among the various units of local government and accepted a modified version of the House's principle of placing restrictions on how local governments could use revenue-sharing funds. Also, the conference committee dropped the Senate provision of $4 billion for supplementary social service grants.

Thus, the concept of general revenue sharing, which had for years been supported by various academic, civic, professional, and political groups, became law on October 20, 1972. In signing the general revenue-sharing bill, President Nixon stated, "The signing today of the State and Local Fiscal Assistance Act of 1972—the legislation known as general revenue sharing—means that this New American Revolution is truly underway. . . . What America wants today, at the State level, at the city level and at the county level, and I believe at the Federal level, is not bigger government, but better government and that is what this is about."[47]

According to the final provisions of the legislation, a total of $30.2 billion, two-thirds of which is to go directly to general purpose local governments, is to be distributed to states and localities over a five-year period. On an annual basis, the amounts of revenue-sharing funds to be distributed are as shown below.

1972: $5.300 billion
1973: $5.975 billion
1974: $6.125 billion
1975: $6.275 billion
1976: $6.425 billion

In determining the precise distribution of the funds, each state is to get the larger appropriation by applying either the House or the Senate formula. Within each state, the bill provides for a four-step process by which the local units of government are to receive their share. That process operates as follows:

Step 1. Each county receives an amount accounting for population, tax effort, and relative income.

Step 2. Each county government receives a share determined by the ratio of its tax collections to tax collections by all governments in the county.

Step 3. All townships within a county receive an amount determined by their relative share of tax collections, and each township's share of this amount is determined by the three-factor formula (accounting for population, tax effort, and relative per capita income).

Step 4. Municipal governments share the remainder according to the three-factor formula (accounting for population, tax effort, and relative per capita income). Tables 3-1 and 3-2 indicate the amount of revenue-sharing funds received by the 50 states and by the 50 largest metropolitan areas in fiscal 1973 according to this formula.

Tables 3-1 and 3-2 indicate that some states and some cities receive larger per capita portions of general revenue sharing than the average, regardless of which formula is applied. As mentioned above, the House formula favors heavily urbanized states, less wealthy states, and those with large tax efforts of their own. The Senate formula favors mainly the poorer states. The states and cities that "lose" in these formulas are those not at the extreme of either formula. Those states such as Connecticut, Illinois, Ohio, Pennsylvania, and Texas, and those cities such as San Diego, Jacksonville, and Rochester receive less per capita than the average because of this.

The act also specifies that general revenue-sharing funds received by units of local government "may be used only for priority expenditures," including public safety, environmental protection, public transportation, health, recreation, libraries, social services for the poor and aged, and financial administration. Such funds may also be used for "ordinary and necessary" capital expenditures. States are not required to use their funds for "priority" items. General revenue-sharing funds may not be used as matching funds for federal grants-in-aid programs and may not be used for any program or project discriminating on the basis of race, color, national origin, or sex. Finally, the law requires that each locality report its use of the funds at a time designated by the Secretary of the Treasury and that these reports be published in a local newspaper.

The most noticeable characteristic of the State and Local Fiscal Assistance Act of 1972 is the absence of detailed restrictions and provisions concerning the spending of returned revenue. Richard Eckfield finds that "In terms of dollars to be spent, this measure has to rank among the simplest, least complicated pieces of legislation to pass Congress in many years. . . . By and large the states and local governments are free to exercise discretion over the use of their funds."[48]

General Revenue Sharing and the New Federalism

As controversial and significant as general revenue sharing is, it should be mentioned that the measure was only one program in President Nixon's broader and perhaps even more controversial package of government reform—that which has been labeled the "New Federalism." Other important programs under his "New Federalism" included proposals for special revenue sharing, federal regional councils, various administrative changes, and suggestions to give mayors access to Highway Trust Fund monies and to give governors authority to integrate Health, Education, Welfare Department social service programs. In terms of legislative and bureaucratic acceptance, general revenue sharing was the most successful of these proposals; however, it is appropriate, for a full understanding of general revenue sharing, to consider it in the much broader context of the philosophy responsible for the "New Federalism" proposals.

In his 1971 State of the Union Address, Nixon proposed that along with general revenue sharing, the Congress also adopt a series of special revenue-sharing measures. At that time, he proposed that Congress make $11 billion dollars in the coming fiscal year available for special revenue-sharing programs in the areas of urban development, rural development, education, transportation, manpower training, and law enforcement. In his Budgetary Message to Congress in 1971 (for fiscal year 1972), President Nixon specified the precise distribution of special revenue-sharing funds as shown below.

Urban Community Development:	$2.0 billion
Rural Community Development:	$1.0 billion
Education:	$3.0 billion
Manpower Training:	$2.0 billion
Law Enforcement:	$ .5 billion
Transportation:	$2.6 billion

Along with general revenue sharing, President Nixon noted that these proposals would make available $16.1 billion to the states and localities in fiscal year 1972. He remarked that "This is about half of Federal Government aid, excluding public assistance grants, to states and communities —a historic and massive reversal of the flow of power in America."[49]

Special revenue sharing, as outlined by President Nixon, differed from general revenue sharing in that it would entail almost no new, additional sources of money for states and localities. Rather, it was Nixon's intent to combine and consolidate categorical grant programs[50] in each of these areas in a way that would allow much greater flexibility in the spending of

Table 3-1
General Revenue-Sharing Funds Received by State Governments: 1973

	Amount of Revenue Sharing	Percent of Total Revenue Sharing	1970 State Population	Percent of U.S. Population	Revenue-Sharing Dollars Per Capita	State Government Share as Percent of State Expenditure
Ala.	$116,100,000	2.2	3,444,165	1.7	$33.70	3.4
Alaska	6,300,000	0.1	300,382	0.1	20.97	0.5
Ariz.	50,200,000	0.9	1,770,900	0.9	28.35	3.0
Ark.	55,000,000	1.0	1,923,295	0.9	28.59	3.7
Calif.	556,100,000	10.5	19,953,134	9.8	27.87	2.6
Colo.	54,600,000	1.0	2,207,259	1.1	24.73	2.5
Conn.	66,200,000	1.2	3,031,709	1.5	21.84	1.6
Del.	15,800,000	0.3	548,104	0.3	28.59	1.8
D.C.	23,600,000	0.4	756,510	0.4	31.26	2.7
Fla.	146,000,000	2.8	6,789,443	3.3	21.50	3.0
Ga.	109,900,000	2.1	4,589,575	2.3	23.94	2.8
Hawaii	23,800,000	0.4	768,561	0.4	30.96	1.1
Idaho	19,900,000	0.4	712,567	0.4	27.92	2.4
Ill.	274,700,000	5.2	11,113,976	5.5	24.71	2.7
Ind.	104,300,000	2.0	5,193,669	2.6	20.08	2.8
Iowa	77,000,000	1.5	2,824,376	1.4	27.26	3.0
Kan.	52,800,000	1.0	2,246,578	1.1	23.50	3.2
Ky.	87,300,000	1.6	3,218,706	1.6	27.12	2.5
La.	113,600,000	2.1	3,641,306	1.8	31.19	2.9
Maine	31,100,000	0.6	992,048	0.5	31.34	2.4
Md.	107,000,000	2.0	3,922,399	1.9	27.27	3.0
Mass.	163,000,000	3.1	5,689,170	2.8	28.65	2.3
Mich.	221,900,000	4.2	8,875,083	4.4	25.00	2.4
Minn.	103,900,000	2.0	3,804,971	1.9	27.30	3.3

Miss.	90,700,000	1.7	2,216,912	1.1	40.91	4.3
Mo.	98,800,000	1.9	4,676,501	2.3	21.12	2.6
Mont.	20,600,000	0.4	694,409	0.3	29.66	2.0
Neb.	42,900,000	0.8	1,483,493	0.7	28.91	4.0
Nev.	11,100,000	0.2	488,738	0.2	22.71	1.8
N.H.	15,200,000	0.3	737,681	0.4	20.60	1.7
N.J.	163,600,000	3.1	7,168,164	3.5	22.82	2.5
N.M.	33,200,000	0.6	1,016,000	0.5	32.67	2.8
N.Y.	591,400,000	11.2	18,236,967	9.0	32.42	3.6
N.C.	135,500,000	2.6	5,082,059	2.5	26.66	3.6
N.D.	19,700,000	0.4	617,761	0.3	31.88	2.6
Ohio	207,000,000	3.9	10,652,017	5.2	19.43	2.4
Okla.	59,400,000	1.1	2,559,229	1.3	23.21	2.2
Ore.	56,200,000	1.1	2,091,385	1.0	26.87	2.1
Pa.	274,000,000	5.2	11,793,909	5.8	23.23	2.0
R.I.	23,600,000	0.4	946,725	0.5	24.92	1.8
S.C.	81,500,000	1.5	2,590,516	1.3	31.46	4.0
S.D.	25,100,000	0.5	665,507	0.3	37.71	3.4
Tenn.	98,400,000	1.9	3,923,687	1.9	25.07	3.1
Tex.	244,500,000	4.6	11,196,730	5.5	21.83	2.9
Utah	31,400,000	0.6	1,059,273	0.5	29.64	2.3
Vt.	14,800,000	0.3	444,330	0.2	33.30	1.7
Va.	105,200,000	2.0	4,648,494	2.3	22.63	2.6
Wash.	84,100,000	1.6	3,409,169	1.7	24.66	1.5
W. Va.	52,300,000	0.9	1,744,237	0.9	29.98	2.2
Wis.	133,900,000	2.5	4,417,731	2.2	30.30	3.5
Wyo.	9,700,000	0.2	332,416	0.2	29.18	1.8

Source: Joint Committee on Internal Revenue Taxation; Census Bureau.

Table 3-2
General Revenue-Sharing Funds Received by 50 Largest Cities: 1973

	Amount of Revenue Sharing	1970 Population	Revenue-Sharing Dollars Per Capita	Revenue Sharing as Percent of City Expenditures
New York	$247,524,126	7,895,563	$31.34	3.1
Chicago	69,477,799	3,369,359	20.62	9.1
Los Angeles	35,422,819	2,809,596	12.61	5.9
Philadelphia	43,758,115	1,950,098	22.44	6.3
Detroit	36,530,556	1,512,893	24.15	8.5
Houston	14,029,925	1,232,802	11.38	9.3
Baltimore	23,881,944	905,759	26.37	3.6
Dallas	9,699,255	844,401	11.49	5.9
Washington, D.C.	23,647,564	756,510	31.26	2.7
Cleveland	14,107,681	750,879	18.79	7.9
Indianapolis	6,983,136	745,739	9.36	5.5
Milwaukee	11,221,768	717,372	15.64	7.2
San Francisco	19,276,751	715,674	26.94	3.9
San Diego	6,527,384	697,027	9.36	5.7
San Antonio	7,785,895	654,153	11.90	12.2
Boston	17,753,054	641,071	27.69	4.1
Memphis	9,826,564	623,530	15.76	4.3
St. Louis	12,702,004	622,236	20.41	7.9
New Orleans	14,744,411	593,471	24.84	12.7
Pheonix	9,280,433	581,562	15.96	10.2
Columbus	5,697,361	540,025	10.55	5.5
Seattle	9,863,462	530,831	18.58	7.4
Jacksonville	3,972,067	528,865	7.51	4.4

Pittsburgh	11,679,788	520,117	22.46	12.0
Denver	12,189,871	514,678	23.68	6.9
Kansas City, Mo.	10,222,093	507,330	20.15	7.8
Atlanta	4,583,171	497,421	9.21	2.8
Buffalo	7,328,071	462,768	15.84	3.4
Cincinnati	8,501,849	452,524	18.79	3.4
Nashville-Davidson	6,378,838	477,877	14.24	3.8
San Jose, Calif.	4,033,602	445,799	9.05	5.0
Minneapolis	4,814,471	434,400	11.08	5.2
Fort Worth	4,207,340	393,476	10.69	7.7
Toledo	4,467,549	383,818	11.64	6.5
Newark	8,437,328	381,930	22.09	4.1
Portland	8,579,738	380,629	22.54	13.4
Oklahoma City	6,783,125	386,856	18.39	11.2
Louisville	9,480,686	361,958	26.19	14.9
Oakland	5,775,003	361,561	15.97	8.1
Long Beach	3,746,725	358,633	10.45	3.3
Omaha	3,640,464	346,929	10.49	7.5
Miami	6,959,236	334,859	20.78	13.4
Tulsa	3,013,250	330,350	9.12	5.9
Honolulu	12,542,903	324,871	38.61	8.4
El Paso	5,473,903	322,261	16.99	17.2
St. Paul	4,450,117	309,828	14.36	5.4
Norfolk	6,740,023	307,951	21.89	4.3
Birmingham	7,099,587	300,910	23.59	16.3
Rochester	2,293,973	296,233	7.74	1.4
Tampa	5,640,879	277,767	20.31	14.5

Source: Joint Committee on Internal Revenue Taxation; Census Bureau.

funds by local governments and would involve much less direct supervision by the federal government. In essence, he was proposing the adoption of the block grant concept in these six areas,[51] and it is this consolidation and elimination of various categorical grant programs that became the most controversial aspect of special revenue sharing.

In a series of proposals in 1971, President Nixon submitted his special revenue-sharing measures to the Congress. His education revenue-sharing bill would have consolidated 33 categorical grant programs and his transportation revenue-sharing bill would have consolidated 23 categorical grant programs. His community development revenue-sharing bill would have consolidated urban renewal, model cities, and water and sewer grant programs. The law enforcement revenue-sharing proposal would have converted what was already a block grant program into a pure no-strings measure, and the rural development revenue-sharing proposal would have consolidated 10 categorical grant programs. The Nixon Administration's manpower revenue-sharing measure would have consolidated more than a dozen categorical grants and would have repealed the Manpower Development and Training Act of 1962 as well as the manpower training section of the Economic Opportunity Act of 1964.[52]

Of course, each of these proposals received considerable opposition. Congress, in particular, proved extremely reluctant to approve measures that it felt would lead to a net reduction of congressional influence. Referring to the categorical grant programs to be eliminated under President Nixon's transportation revenue-sharing proposal, Transportation Under Secretary James Beggs stated: "Our categorical programs are nearer and dearer to congressmen's hearts than any other. They are the porkiest of the pork and Congress guards them jealously."[53]

As of this writing, only the manpower and housing-community development measures have been enacted. As passed by Congress in December 1973, the Comprehensive Employment and Training Act (CETA) does give mayors and governors increased decision-making authority in local manpower programs; however, it accounts for only 40 percent of the annual $4.8 billion federal manpower outlays. Also, the act, itself, continues some categorical grant programs. The Job Corps is continued as a separate national program, and separate federal efforts are authorized for migrants, youth, non-English-speaking persons, and American Indians. In fact, over a third of the 1975 CETA budget will be spent on these "categorical" programs. In spite of these restrictions, state and local officials will have a large degree of freedom in allocating the remaining two-thirds of CETA funds.[54]

The other special revenue-sharing proposals did not fare as well. The Nixon Administration, itself, dropped the rural community development and transportation revenue-sharing requests. Transportation was dropped, the Nixon Administration explained, because its purpose would be served by proposals to open the highway trust funds for mass transportation programs; rural development was dropped because of the passage of the Rural Development Act of 1972, which provided authorization to start programs "consistent with the revenue-sharing concept."[55] In law enforcement, the Nixon Administration did not continue to push its special revenue-sharing proposal.

In his 1971 State of the Union Address, President Nixon also called for a "sweeping reorganization of the executive branch." Accordingly, he proposed the reduction of the present 12 cabinet departments to 8. He suggested that the Departments of State, Treasury, Defense, and Justice remain, but that all the others be consolidated into 4: Human Resources, Community Development, Natural Resources, and Economic Development. Under this plan, Nixon said, "rather than dividing up our departments by narrow subjects, we would organize them around the great purposes of government. Rather than scattering responsibility by adding new levels of bureaucracy, we would focus and concentrate the responsibility for getting problems solved. With these four departments, when we have a problem we will know where to go—and the department will have the authority and the resources to do something about it."[56] Of these reorganization proposals, Congress seriously considered only the creation of the Community Development Department. Although the bill passed the Senate, it died in the House.

President Nixon was more successful in 1969 in creating common regional boundaries for major domestic departments and agencies. Following his directives, the bulk of the domestic federal agencies now operate from 10 regional offices located in Atlanta, Boston, Chicago, Dallas, Denver, Kansas City, New York, Philadelphia, San Francisco, and Seattle. At the center of each of these are the Federal Regional Councils, comprised of representatives of 7 federal agencies—Housing and Urban Development, Health, Education, and Welfare, Labor, Transportation, the Office of Economic Opportunity, the Environmental Protection Agency, and the Law Enforcement Assistance Administration. These councils are to assist state and local governments in program planning, administration, and evaluation.

"New Federalism," then, was to have included broad federal and administrative reorganization changes. Full implementation of President Nixon's proposals would have meant the enactment of a series of special revenue-sharing measures and sweeping executive and administrative changes as well as the passage of general revenue sharing. Perhaps the best summary of the basic principles of the "New Federalism" has been provided by Richard Nathan. In his testimony before the Senate Subcommittee on Intergovernmental Relations of the Committee on Government

Operations, Nathan outlined seven tenets of the "New Federalism" philosophy. These include:

1. Income transfers to people should be given greater emphasis as the main way to help the poor.

2. Human services programs to aid the poor and others who should be eligible are activities that should be regarded as primarily state-local functions.

3. Community service programs are predominantly state-local functions where federal financial assistance should be provided on a broad basis according to community needs.

4. Certain broad inter-area environmental functions where problems or needs spill over to a significant degree among regions are fields of government activity where federal intervention is appropriate.

5. Research and the dissemination of research findings on public problems is appropriately a national government responsibility.

6. In areas in which it is determined should be regarded as primarily state-local, the strong emphasis of federal financial assistance policies should be to encourage political accountability by elected general government officials (governors, mayors, county executives, and state-local legislators).

7. In areas of public activity where governmental responsibilities are not well established, categorical grants are appropriate to encourage the development of these services, although on the assumption that they will later be phased out as state and local governments take on these functions.[57]

Much of the opposition to President Nixon's "New Federalism" proposals emanated from those same groups and organizations opposed to general revenue sharing, as discussed above. These organizations and their motives need not be reviewed again here; however, a particular interesting opponent to elements of the "New Federalism" package was Walter Heller—one of the original proponents of revenue sharing in the early 1960s. Heller, it will be recalled from the discussion in Chapter 2, proposed revenue sharing as an *additive* source of funds for state and local governments. In his 1973 testimony before the Senate Subcommittee on Intergovernmental Relations of the Committee on Government Operations, Heller was particularly critical of what he perceived to be proposals by President Nixon for the *substitution* of revenue-sharing money for on-going categorical grant programs. In his testimony, Dr. Heller stated:

Mr. Nixon has a short memory about the purposes and the pledges involved in the birth and gestation period of general revenue sharing. After all, it was conceived to fill a gap in the family of Federal fiscal supports to State and local governments . . .

The President is proposing [in his fiscal-1974 budget] to encumber it to support functions that really are suffused with the national interest and ought to be supported directly by categorical aids.[58]

Testifying before that same committee, Mayor Moon Landrieu of New Orleans also expressed considerable disappointment in the elimination of many categorical grant programs from the president's 1974 budget. After having been assured that general revenue sharing was to be an additional source of funds, "Imagine our shock," Mayor Landrieu stated, "our dismay, our confusion, and our anger, when the budget was released calling for no money for Model Cities, a token amount for urban renewal, and an end to numerous categorical programs. Our shock was further compounded when we saw that the section of the budget providing for the dismantling of OEO also contains the following language: 'If constituencies of individual communities desire to continue providing financial support to local community action agencies, general and special revenue-sharing funds could be used.'"[59]

Thus, President Nixon's "New Federalism" proposals involved much more than simply his general revenue-sharing program. Like general revenue sharing, opposition to "New Federalism" centered around congressional fears of loss of power and concerns by many, such as Mayor Landrieu and Professor Heller, of the consequences of the phasing out of various categorical grant programs.

Conclusion

After having received support from both political parties, academicians as well as politicians, liberals as well as conservatives, general revenue sharing was finally passed into law in October 1972. Much of the credit for its passage was due to its endorsement by President Nixon who, himself, had never held a local or state elective office. Even with Nixon's strong support, the measure faced stiff congressional opposition and was passed only after intensive lobbying efforts on the part of many state and local government organizations.

General revenue sharing, it is stressed, must be viewed in the broader context of Nixon's entire "New Federalism" program. The enactment of this full range of proposals would have meant, according to Nixon, "A New American Revolution—a peaceful revolution in which power is turned back to the people . . . a revolution as profound, as far-reaching, as exciting as that first revolution almost 200 years ago," and that in "just five years America [can] enter its third century as a young nation, new in spirit, with all the vigor and the freshness with which it began its first century."[60]

Despite the president's support for his "New Federalism" proposals, only general revenue sharing was to survive largely intact when the legislative process was complete. As the following chapters indicate, an analysis of the impact of the general revenue-sharing measure provides some insight into the possible consequences that the entire "New Federalism" program would have in the future of American politics.

Notes

1. The "new American revolution" was the term used by President Nixon in describing his "New Federalism" concept when signing the general revenue-sharing bill in Philadelphia on October 20, 1972. The text of his remarks can be found in *Weekly Compilation of Presidential Documents* (Washington, D.C.: Government Printing Office, 1972), October 23, 1972, pp. 1534-6.

2. This "fiscal crisis" is discussed in Chapter 2.

3. See: *National Journal,* December 16, 1972, p. 1916, for a full discussion of the Administration's philosophy.

4. Richard E. Thompson, *Revenue Sharing: A New Era in Federalism?* (Washington, D.C.: Revenue Sharing Advisory Service, 1973), p. 38.

5. President Nixon's 1971 State of the Union Message may be found in *Public Papers of the Presidents of the United States: Richard Nixon* (Washington, D.C.: Government Printing Office, 1972), January 22, 1971.

6. Quoted in *National Journal,* December 16, 1972, p. 1916.

7. Quoted in *CQ Guide To Current American Government* (Washington, D.C.: Congressional Quarterly Inc., 1974), p. 47.

8. Thompson, *Revenue Sharing: A New Era in Federalism?,* pp. 39-40.

9. Alan Beals, "Revenue Sharing: Has Its Time Finally Come?" *Nations Cities* 9 (January 1971), pp. 11-13.

10. A detailed discussion of this phase of the revenue-sharing legislation may be found in *National Review,* April 3, 1971, pp. 712-3.

11. These organizations include the National League of Cities, the United States Conference of Mayors, International City Management Association, National Association of Counties, National Governors' Conference, Council of State Governments, and National Legislative Conference. The legislative lobbying tactics of these organizations are discussed in more detail in a later section of this chapter.

12. As reported in Thompson, *Revenue Sharing: A New Era in Federalism?,* p. 60.

13. Reported in *National Journal,* April 3, 1971, p. 712.

14. Reported in Beals, "Revenue Sharing: Has Its Time Finally Come?" p. 13.

15. *National Journal,* April 3, 1971, p. 712.

16. President Nixon's *Annual Message to the Congress on the State of the Union,* January 22, 1971.

17. Ibid.

18. Details of this plan may be found in *1972 Congressional Quarterly Almanac* (Washington, D.C.: Congressional Quarterly Inc., 1972), p. 638; and *National Journal,* April 3, 1971, pp. 715-6.

19. Ibid.

20. As reported in "Congress Clears Nixon's Revenue-Sharing Plan," *1972 Congressional Quarterly Almanac,* p. 645.

21. Reported in *New York Times,* January 26, 1971.

22. U.S. Congress, House, Committee on Ways and Means, *General Revenue Sharing,* 92nd Congress, 1st Sess., June 2 and 3, 1971, 51, pp. 169-70.

23. As reported in National League of Cities, *Support your City, Support Revenue Sharing* (Washington, D.C.: National League of Cities, 1972), p. 4.

24. Ibid.

25. Ibid., pp. 305.

26. "Congress Clears Nixon's Revenue-Sharing Plan," *1972 Congressional Quarterly Almanac,* p. 642.

27. Quoted in *National Journal,* October 7, 1972, p. 1561.

28. Quoted in ibid., p. 1562.

29. U.S. Congress, House, Committee on Ways and Means, *General Revenue Sharing,* pp. 918-20 (emphasis added).

30. Quoted in *National Journal,* April 10, 1971, p. 771.

31. The most complete account of this opposition may be found in *National Journal,* April 10, 1971, p. 771. Much of the following is taken from this discussion.

32. Ibid.

33. 1971 resolution of the National Association for the Advancement of Colored People, as provided to the authors by J. Francis Pohlacs, counsel, National Association for the Advancement of Colored People.

34. The best discussion of the role of these organizations in the passage of general revenue sharing may be found in Thompson, *Revenue Sharing: A New Era in Federalism?,* pp. 45-54.

35. Ibid., p. 48.

36. U.S. Congress, House, Committee on Ways and Means, *General Revenue Sharing*, p. 237.

37. Ibid., p. 242.

38. Ibid., p. 243.

39. Thompson, *Revenue Sharing: A New Era in Federalism?*, p. 76.

40. Ibid., p. 77.

41. Ibid., p. 86.

42. President Nixon's Annual Message to the Congress on the State of the Union, January 29, 1972 may be found in *Weekly Compilation of Presidential Documents* (Washington, D.C.: Government Printing Office, 1972), p. 74.

43. As reported in "Congress Clears Nixon's Revenue-Sharing Plan," in *1972 Congressional Quarterly Almanac*, p. 639.

44. A more complete discussion of the revenue-sharing bill as it emerged from the House Ways and Means Committee can be found in *1972 Congressional Quarterly Almanac*, pp. 639-40.

45. Ibid., p. 640.

46. Quoted in ibid., p. 641.

47. The full text of President Nixon's written and oral remarks when signing the general revenue-sharing bill in Philadelphia, October 20, 1972 may be found in *Weekly Compilation of Presidential Documents* (Washington, D.C.: Government Printing Office), October 23, 1972, pp. 1534-7.

48. Richard E. Eckfield, *Management Guide to Revenue Sharing*, Management Information Service Report, Vol. 4, No. 11, November 1972 (Washington, D.C.: International City Management Association, 1972), p. 1.

49. Annual Budget Message to the Congress, Fiscal Year 1972, January 29, 1971, found in *Public Papers of the Presidents* (Washington, D.C.: Government Printing Office, 1972).

50. For a discussion of categorical grant programs see Chapter 2.

51. For a discussion of block grant programs see Chapter 2.

52. An in-depth discussion of these proposals may be found in *National Journal*, December 16, 1972, pp. 1927-31.

53. Quoted in ibid., p. 1928.

54. An analysis of this bill may be found in "The Comprehensive Employment and Training Act: Opportunities and Challenges, A Position Paper" (Washington, D.C.: National Manpower Task Force, 1974).

55. Reported in *CQ Guide to Current American Government*, p. 49.

56. President Nixon's Annual Message to the Congress on the State of the Union, January 22, 1971.

57. U.S. Congress, Senate Subcommittee on Intergovernmental Relations of the Committee on Government Operations, *A New Federalism,* 93rd Cong., 1st Sess., February 23, 1973, pp. 96-97. It should be noted that Nathan emphasized in his testimony that he spoke only for himself and not on behalf of President Nixon or the Administration.

58. Walter Heller in ibid., p. 74.

59. Mayor Moon Landrieu in ibid., February 21, 1973, p. 11.

60. President Nixon's Annual Message to the Congress on the State of the Union, January 22, 1971.

General Revenue Sharing and City Expenditure Decisions

Introduction

Certainly one of the most important aspects of general revenue sharing is how the funds are being spent by the recipient units of government. As Congressman L. H. Fountain of North Carolina has remarked, "General revenue sharing is essentially unconditional aid which may be spent with a minimum of federal control."[1] There has been and will continue to be considerable discussion over how the general revenue-sharing funds should be spent as well as how the funds are actually being spent. As discussed in Chapter 2, Congressman Henry Reuss, among others, has advocated the funds be used to promote governmental reform,[2] and the task of identifying how the funds are actually being used is not simple.

As mentioned earlier, cities are restricted to using their funds for "priority" items or any ordinary and necessary capital expenditure items, and they are required to file periodic reports on the planned and actual use of their funds with the Office of Revenue Sharing.[3] Most economists would contend that because the general revenue-sharing funds are highly fungible, these formal reports are not necessarily accurate indicators of how the funds are being used because they do not indicate what happens to the funds being replaced. Thus, for example, a city can report that its general revenue-sharing funds are going to police and fire protection, while the funds normally allocated from local sources for these expenditures may go to education or other items that are not on the "priority" list. In this case, then, the "impact" of general revenue sharing would be in education, not public safety. Because of this possibility, Congressman Fountain summarized the view of many when he stated:

Despite the statutory requirements that local governments restrict their expenditure of shared revenues to certain high priorities and report on the uses of this money, there is little likelihood of identifying the actual impact of these expenditures with any degree of certainty. This is so because these funds are often substituted for local money which is then used for purposes unrelated to the expenditure categories specified in the law.[4]

At a conference held in December 1972 by the National Planning Association and the National Science Foundation, a wide variety of approaches for the study of general revenue-sharing decisions were

67

considered.[5] In order to deal with the fungibility characteristic, a variety of research methodologies have been adopted and implemented. In addition to the questionnaire and survey research approaches, the most popular has been a case study approach. Of these, the on-going study "Monitoring Revenue Sharing" being conducted by the Brookings Institution is the most comprehensive.[6] The Brookings' project is a five-year study ". . . to determine how cities and states use the $30.2 billion received through the revenue-sharing program."[7] The project uses 20 field observers in approximately 70 jurisdictions; the field observer's task is to monitor the governmental unit's decision-making process as it relates to general revenue-sharing funds.

Another major revenue-sharing research project involves the League of Women Voters Education Fund, the Center for Community Change, the Center for National Policy Review, and the National Urban Coalition, all of which have joined together to ". . . monitor and evaluate general revenue sharing during the next two years, and will encourage citizen participation in the allocation and distribution of the funds."[8] Approximately 70 units of government will be included in this project, and in this case, the objective is not only to monitor, but to increase citizen knowledge and ultimate impact on the expenditure decisions reached for general revenue-sharing funds.

The above discussion is intended to point out that there are indeed a variety of approaches to the study of general revenue-sharing decisions, but that no one approach satisfies the many methodological problems confronting the researcher interested in investigating as complex and complicated a program as general revenue sharing. Any case study approach is subject to the criticisms of inapplicability to other units and the problem of comparative reliability when a variety of researchers are involved. Revenue-sharing research, as the program itself, should be adaptive and imaginative. It is our hope that the variety of research methodologies will increase and that the dissemination and comparison of the results will be carried out by all interested parties.

This study is based on questionnaires mailed in January of 1973 and 1974 to each chief executive in cities over 50,000 in 1970.[a] Table 4-1 summarizes the response rate by various types of cities for both surveys. The response rate was obtained after only one mailing; it was sufficiently high and representative to preclude additional mailings of the same questionnaire. As the responses indicate, there were no major gaps in the response rates, which thus increases our confidence in generalizing from the respondents to all cities in the categories. The lowest response rates for the 1973 survey—except for cities with "other" form of government

---

[a]See Appendix A for a copy of the questionnaires and a complete description of the research strategy utilized.

Table 4-1
Questionnaire Response Rates

Classification	No. of Cities Surveyed (A)	Cities Responding 1973 No.	Cities Responding 1973 (% of A)	Cities Responding 1974 No.	Cities Responding 1974 (% of A)
Total, All Cities	409	213	52.1	216	52.8
Population Group					
Over 500,000	26	14	53.8	13	50.0
250,000 to 500,000	30	19	63.3	21	70.0
100,000 to 250,000	98	56	57.1	60	61.2
50,000 to 100,000	255	124	48.6	122	47.8
Metropolitan Type[a]					
Central City	258	138	53.5	137	53.1
Suburban	151	75	49.7	71	47.0
Region[a]					
Northeast	99	40	40.4	48	48.5
North Central	106	58	54.7	58	54.7
South	101	60	59.4	52	51.5
West	93	55	59.1	50	53.8
Form of Government[a]					
Mayor-Council	164	74	45.1	66	40.2
Council-Manager	212	126	59.4	122	57.5
Other	31	13	41.9	19	61.3

[a]Not all cities could be coded on this variable due to incomplete information.

—were cities in the Northeast (40.4 percent); mayor-council cities (45.1 percent); cities in the 50,000 to 100,000 population group (48.6 percent); and suburban cities (49.7 percent). For the 1974 survey, only mayor-council cities (40.2 percent); suburban cities (47.0 percent); cities in the 50,000 to 100,000 category (47.8 percent) and Northeastern cities (48.5 percent) had response rates less than 50 percent. While conducting mail questionnaires, extensive time went into coding a variety of political, socioeconomic, and demographic data for each of the 409 cities over 50,000. Data included the 1971 budgetary expenditures for each city,[9] municipal government organization (form of government, partisan or non-partisan, and method of council election),[10] and census information (population variables such as size, population change, percent non-white, mean income, and foreign stock).[11] In addition, information on each city's regional location and type (central versus suburban) was coded. The result, by late Spring 1973, was a large file for each of the 409 cities. The file has been and will continue to be expanded as additional data for each city becomes available.

Expenditure Decisions

How the $30.2 billion in general revenue-sharing funds is expended has been and will continue to be a prime question for observers of the program. As already discussed, the legislative debate over the program was often intense, and a variety of claims as to the effects of the program were made. Certainly members of Congress hold quite different perspectives of the intent of general revenue sharing, and these differences, even after the legislation had been in effect for over 11 months, were still apparent in a survey conducted by the Intergovernmental Relations Subcommittee of the House of Representatives.[12] Add to this not only the perspectives of local officials attempting to provide services as well as to survive politically but also the needs of various community groups from police to welfare recipients and it soon becomes obvious why general revenue sharing tends to have such diverse meanings to its various observers and participants. The remaining portions of this chapter analyze the expenditure decisions reached by the respondents during the first four entitlement periods. Approximately 50 percent of the $30.2 billion had been allocated by this point, and the trends had become discernible.

Table 4-2 summarizes the expenditures by categories for the 213 responding cities in 1973 and the 216 responding cities in 1974 and compares those expenditures with the respondents' expenditure decisions during the 1971 budgetary year, which was the last full budgetary year prior to general revenue sharing.

As is indicated in Table 4-2, 53 percent of initial general revenue-sharing funds was allocated in 1973 to environmental protection, street and road repair, law enforcement, fire prevention, and parks and recreation. A small proportion of funds was allocated to social and health services, while nearly a fifth (18.8 percent) of the funds had not been allocated. There are several possible explanations for the initial expenditure patterns.

First, note that the initial general revenue-sharing expenditures closely parallel those of the 1971 budgetary year. Law enforcement, street and road repair, health, parks and recreation, and libraries received a slightly smaller proportion of general revenue-sharing funds than in the previous budgetary year while the others received somewhat more. The important point is that the differences between prior budgetary allocations and initial general revenue expenditure decisions are not large. This supports the contention that since the initial funds arrived late in the budgetary decision-making process (in some cases, even after the budget had been set), many cities simply allocated the initial funds in similar proportion to their prior budgetary totals. This would certainly be consistent with those who maintain that local budgeting is largely incremental in nature.[13]

Another possible explanation is that since many city officials felt they

Table 4-2
Prior Budgetary and General Revenue-Sharing Expenditures (%) in Cities over 50,000

Expenditure Category	General Revenue-Sharing Expenditures 1973 (N = 213) %	Prior Budgetary Expenditures[a] 1971 (N = 213) %	General Revenue-Sharing Expenditures 1974 (N = 216) %	Prior Budgetary Expenditures[a] 1971 (N = 216) %
Law Enforcement	11.3	13.3	16.3	12.6
Fire Prevention	10.3	10.0	15.3	9.4
Building and Code Enforcement	1.4	NA	.7	NA
Environmental Protection	12.6	11.9	13.2	11.8
Transit Systems	1.9	NA	2.9	NA
Street and Road Repair	11.6	11.9	12.5	11.6
Social Services	1.7	1.0	2.8	1.1
Health	1.5	3.5	2.8	3.7
Parks and Recreation	7.2	7.4	10.9	6.9
Building Renovation	4.0	3.8	3.9	3.7
Libraries	1.4	2.0	2.2	1.9
Municipal Salaries	4.3	NA	1.1	NA
Other	12.0	35.2	11.3	37.3
Undetermined	18.8	NA	4.1	NA
Totals	100.0	100.0	100.0	100.0

[a]Analysis, in addition to that reported here, was done by removing education from total expenditures and then dividing the new expenditure total into the amount spent in each category. There were no significant differences when this was done.

Source: 1971 budgetary expenditures calculated from data in Table 5, U.S. Bureau of the Census, *City Government Finances in 1970-1971* (Washington, D.C.: Government Printing Office, 1972).

were faced with a critical fiscal situation late 1972, initial general revenue-sharing decisions were dictated by the need to continue and strengthen, if possible, already existing programs. Thus, priorities remained the same.

The 1974 results indicate that a different pattern may be developing, since 68.2 percent of the funds were allocated for the same five functions (law enforcement, fire prevention, environmental protection, street and road repair, and parks and recreation). In all five cases, this represented an increase in the level of funding over the 1971 budgetary year. The law enforcement, fire prevention and parks and recreation categories had size-able proportional increases. Most of this increase may be due to the substantial decrease in the proportion of funds "undetermined" in 1974 as compared to 1973. Regardless of the reasons, cities had allocated their funds much more quickly in 1974 as the 4.1 percent in the undetermined category indicates. This reflects the "cycling in" of the general revenue-sharing funds to the cities' regular budgetary decision-making process.

Based on Table 4-2, it is obvious which expenditure categories have fared well in amounts of general revenue-sharing funds received. It is also apparent that health and social services, even though the social services category received a greater proportion of general revenue-sharing funds than it had in prior budgetary years, have not received large proportions of general revenue-sharing funds.

At least one possible explanation why cities have allocated revenue-sharing funds as they have may be due to the strong bargaining position of the police and fire organizations in the various communities.[14] It would be logically consistent to conclude that well-organized leadership and experience in the budgetary decision-making process may result in large allocations of general revenue-sharing funds. Police, fire, parks and recreation, environmental protection advocates of expenditures for sewerage and water quality, and streets and highways personnel have had long experience in dealing with local political leaders. It would be unrealistic to assume that such groups would not get a large share, at least initially, of any new revenues that came to the city.

At the same time, interest groups promoting stronger or expanded social and health services may have tended in previous years to rely more heavily upon federal funding for their programs. This is especially true of low-income and many non-white areas that used federal poverty program, Model City, and urban renewal funds to develop and augment existing city services. Suddenly the "arena" for budgetary politics was changed, and these groups may have lacked the ability to participate as effectively at the local level as other groups with greater experience or power in local politics. If this is in fact the case, it should be expected that the proportion of funds going to social and health services will increase as the local interests become better organized and more effective in influencing the local budgetary process.

This hypothesis is partially confirmed when the results of the 1973 and 1974 survey are compared; both health and social services received larger proportions of general revenue-sharing funds in 1974 than in 1973. However, these conclusions are moderated by the obvious fact that other local expenditure proportions tended to grow as rapidly as those for social and health services.

The full impact of increased citizen participation and awareness should be felt by 1975. Both the League of Women Voters and the Office of Revenue Sharing have attempted to develop and encourage local participation through a series of organizational and informational means.[15] The emphasis has been to explain the revenue-sharing requirements and procedures to the general public in such a way as to encourage interaction and involvement on the assumption that such knowledge will lead to greater effectiveness in gaining revenue-sharing funds.

As Chapter 1 pointed out, the locus of decision making may be critical to which groups receive various benefits. As was discussed, advocates of revenue sharing and fiscal decentralization assume that decentralization is valuable because it will permit local organizations and groups to either influence decision makers or develop the political power necessary to influence them. The problem is threefold: (1) in many cases, local organizations may lack a sufficient power base to influence local budgetary decisions; (2) it may take a considerable length of time, due to the varieties of municipal elections, for local groups to develop such power; and (3) even if the groups are able to organize and develop some power potential, the political system may simply be closed or unresponsive to them. Examples of all three possibilities immediately come to light and should result in a careful review of one's position on this point, which will be fully discussed in Chapters 6 and 7.

While this broad overview of the revenue-sharing decisions may be helpful, it does not permit the more specific questions to be answered. For instance, do expenditure patterns differ as city characteristics differ? If so, how? Certainly one of the major assumptions of advocates of general revenue sharing is that the program permits local decision makers to be more responsive to local needs and desires.[16] If this is in fact the case, different expenditure patterns should develop as city characteristics change.

Revenue-Sharing Expenditure Decisions and City Size, Type, and Region

The following analysis examines the expenditure of general revenue sharing funds "controlling for" those demographic variables found to be significant by previous students of urban policy making and those most applicable to the concerns expressed in the general city expenditure and revenue-sharing literature and debate.[17] Tables 4-3 to 4-5 summarize 1973 and 1974 revenue-sharing decisions by city size, type, and region.

Size has often been cited as one of the more important variables affecting city expenditure decisions.[18] It is usually argued that large cities, especially those over 500,000, are so unique that descriptions usually applied to cities in general must be redefined before being applicable to such large cities.[19] In addition, several of the most active leaders in the urban coalition wanting revenue-sharing legislation were large city mayors. Kevin White of Boston and Wes Uhlman of Seattle were two examples.

A related point raised in Chapter 2 was the fiscal plight of American cities, especially the large ones in the late 1960s and early 1970s.[20] Urban America had just experienced an unprecedented wave of violence, and the larger cities were caught in a seemingly vise-like situation of increased citizen demands and needs at a time when local revenue resources were limited. Property tax rates soared and city leaders regularly complained about impossible budgetary situations and the fact that more services were being demanded at a time of decreasing resources.

If city size does have an independent effect on city expenditure patterns, Table 4-3 should exhibit some of the characteristics attributable to that effect. Table 4-3 does show that for 1973, large cities (those over 250,000) tended to spend a greater proportion of their revenue-sharing funds on law enforcement and fire prevention than did other cities. Cities over 500,000 also spent a larger proportion on building and code enforcement and health services than did other cities. Social services did not receive a large proportion in any size category, with cities in the 250,000 to 500,000 category allocating the smallest proportion of funds (.7 percent) to social services. Environmental protection and street and road repair proportions exhibited varied results. If larger cities did indeed have greater demands for their funds, it was not reflected in the proportions unallocated as cities in the 50,000 to 100,000 category had a larger proportion of unallocated funds (20.4 percent) than those cities over 500,000 (17.2 percent), while cities in the 250,000 to 500,000 category had the largest unexpended proportion (26.3 percent). Based on the 1973 results, it appears that the main impact of city size was to increase the proportion spent on law enforcement and fire prevention.

The pattern is inconsistent for the 1974 returns. With a single exception for each expenditure category, the proportion of city expenditures for law enforcement and fire prevention expenditures increased as size increased. Compared with 1973 allocations, social services did receive larger proportions as size increased, with the cities in the over 500,000 category allocating the largest proportion (5.3 percent). The largest cities also allocated the greatest proportion for environmental protection (19.9 percent) and the

Table 4-3
General Revenue-Sharing Expenditures and City Size

Expenditure Category	1973 Survey (N = 212)				1974 Survey (N = 216)			
	50,000 to 100,000 (N = 124) %	100,000 to 250,000 (N = 56) %	250,000 to 500,000 (N = 19) %	Over 500,000 (N = 13) %	50,000 to 100,000 (N = 122) %	100,000 to 250,000 (N = 60) %	250,000 to 500,000 (N = 21) %	Over 500,000 (N = 13) %
Law Enforcement	10.7	8.6	13.5	22.7	17.2	11.8	19.3	24.1
Fire Prevention	9.9	9.0	14.0	13.3	15.0	15.9	12.7	19.7
Building and Code Enforcement	1.6	.7	.3	4.1	.8	.4	.7	.3
Environmental Protection	12.7	14.9	7.7	10.4	12.8	14.0	9.6	19.9
Transit Systems	1.0	2.0	1.2	4.5	3.3	2.7	2.9	.9
Street and Road Repair	11.1	12.0	13.6	8.3	13.2	12.8	10.3	8.5
Social Services	1.9	1.7	.7	1.7	1.9	4.3	2.5	5.3
Health	1.6	1.2	1.2	2.2	2.6	3.1	2.7	2.8
Parks and Recreation	7.4	8.1	4.0	7.6	11.8	9.7	10.9	6.3
Building Renovation	5.0	2.5	2.0	3.9	4.9	2.6	3.7	.9
Libraries	.8	1.6	.7	0.8	2.3	2.3	.7	1.8
Municipal Salaries	3.4	3.7	9.2	1.6	.7	.5	5.6	1.0
Other	12.5	20.0	5.6	1.7	8.4	16.9	17.0	5.0
Undetermined	20.4	14.0	26.3	17.2	5.1	3.0	1.4	3.5
Total	100.0	100.0	100.0	100.0	100.0	100.0	100.0	100.0

smallest proportion (5.0 percent) for "other" expenditures. It is also found that all the cities allocated their 1974 funds much faster than previously. One other relationship deserves mention: as city size increases, the proportion of funds allocated for street and road repair decreases. Interestingly, the same relationship holds for transit system expenditures, except for the cities in the 250,000 to 500,000 range.

The data in Table 4-3 does not support sweeping generalizations that revenue-sharing expenditure decisions are dictated by size. A consistent pattern over both years appears only in the case of law enforcement and fire prevention. Size may aggravate a variety of conditions, but it appears that this variable alone does not explain the total variation in expenditure decisions.

Another variable often used in conjunction with city size is city type.[21] The usual contention is that type of city helps to determine expenditure patterns with central cities allocating a larger proportion of their expenditures to law enforcement and fire prevention, while suburban cities will allocate a larger proportion of their funds to parks and recreation and environmental protection needs.[22] Table 4-4 offers some interesting data regarding the effect of city type on revenue-sharing decision patterns. Suburban cities spent a larger proportion (11.9 percent in 1973 and 19.7 percent in 1974) on law enforcement than did central cities (10.9 percent in 1973 and 15.0 percent in 1974). The reverse was true regarding fire prevention; central cities (12.6 percent in 1973 and 16.4 percent in 1974) spent a greater proportion on fire prevention than did suburbs (6.1 percent in 1973 and 13.3 percent in 1974). Possible explanations for this may include the suburbanite's increased concern over crime and the central cities' decisions to use general revenue-sharing funds to augment fire prevention expenditures.

Among the other possible comparisons, several are worth noting. Suburban cities spent decidedly more for parks and recreation (9.9 percent in 1973 and 14.8 percent in 1974) than did central cities (5.8 percent in 1973 and 8.9 percent in 1974). Environmental protection allocations remained about the same regardless of city type in both years, while central cities spent a greater proportion on transit systems in 1973 than suburbs. However, this was reversed in 1974 when suburbs spent a larger proportion (3.3 percent to 2.8 percent) on transit systems than did central cities. The categories of social and health services reveal similar patterns with neither type of city allocating a large proportion of their funds to either category. It would seem, then, that city type was not responsible for widely varying expenditure decisions, but that there was some fluctuation in several categories over the two-year period.

Region is another variable often used to explain expenditure patterns.[23] Since rapidly growing cities are found primarily in the South and West,

Table 4-4
General Revenue-Sharing Expenditures and City Type

Expenditure Category	1973 Survey		1974 Survey	
	Central (N = 137) %	Suburban (N = 75) %	Central (N = 137) %	Suburban (N = 71) %
Law Enforcement	10.9	11.9	15.0	19.7
Fire Prevention	12.6	6.1	16.4	13.3
Building and Code Enforcement	1.4	.8	.8	.6
Environmental Protection	12.6	12.7	13.8	11.7
Transit Systems	2.6	.5	2.8	3.3
Street and Road Repair	11.8	10.7	14.0	9.4
Social Services	1.4	2.0	2.6	3.4
Health	1.7	.2	2.7	3.0
Parks and Recreation	5.8	9.9	8.9	14.8
Building Renovation	3.4	4.6	3.4	2.7
Libraries	1.6	1.0	1.7	3.1
Municipal Salaries	3.8	4.7	1.6	.3
Other	11.9	15.7	13.5	8.2
Undetermined	18.5	19.2	2.8	6.5
Total	100.0	100.0	100.0	100.0

some observers have contended that these regional differences result in expenditure pattern differentials.[24] Table 4-5 summarizes the regional expenditure patterns for both surveys. Of the variables investigated so far, region offers the most complex set of results. Cities in the Northeast allocated the largest proportion of funds (16.7 percent in 1973 and 25.6 percent in 1974) to law enforcement, while cities in the South actually allocated a smaller proportion to law enforcement in 1974 than in 1973 (7.8 percent in 1973 and 6.5 percent in 1974). The same pattern holds true for fire prevention expenditures and would seem to indicate that regional expenditures for these items may be related to the strength of unionization with police and fire being most highly unionized in the Northeast, North Central and Western states while being least unionized in the Southern states.[25] In the case of cities in the Northeast, the total proportion allocated for law enforcement and fire prevention exceeded 54 percent of the total revenue-sharing funds received in 1974. In North Central and Western cities in 1974, the proportion exceeded 30 percent of the total revenue-sharing funds, while in the Southern states the proportion represented 13.6 percent of total revenue-sharing funds.

Environmental protection and street and road repair expenditures also are interesting. Cities in the South allocated the largest proportion to both environmental protection (16.4 percent in 1973 and 16.9 percent in 1974) and street and road repair (18.2 percent in 1973 and 19.8 percent in 1974).

Table 4-5
General Revenue-Sharing Expenditures and Region

Expenditure Category	1973 Survey				1974 Survey			
	Northeast (N = 40) %	North Central (N = 58) %	South (N = 60) %	West (N = 55) %	Northeast (N = 48) %	North Central (N = 58) %	South (N = 52) %	West (N = 50) %
Law Enforcement	16.7	11.3	7.8	11.2	25.6	14.2	6.5	21.2
Fire Prevention	15.9	10.0	8.9	8.0	29.0	16.6	7.1	9.3
Building and Code Enforcement	.2	.3	.3	4.8	.2	1.1	.3	1.2
Environmental Protection	14.6	12.6	16.4	7.1	13.2	14.8	16.9	7.0
Transit Systems	.9	1.6	2.2	2.4	1.9	3.5	3.0	3.3
Street and Road Repair	6.9	8.6	18.2	10.8	5.4	12.2	19.8	11.8
Social Services	1.7	2.0	.4	2.8	2.1	4.9	1.1	3.1
Health	1.4	1.1	.8	2.8	6.5	1.9	2.9	.4
Parks and Recreation	3.5	4.2	8.7	11.5	5.5	8.9	10.1	19.1
Building Renovation	1.4	2.8	4.1	7.0	.4	3.6	4.7	4.1
Libraries	1.0	.4	1.5	2.5	1.4	1.0	2.0	4.2
Municipal Salaries	4.4	4.5	3.9	4.3	-0-	.8	3.0	.5
Other	23.0	15.4	11.7	.5	7.6	14.0	16.4	8.7
Undetermined	8.4	25.2	15.1	24.3	1.2	2.5	6.2	6.1
Total	100.0	100.0	100.0	100.0	100.0	100.0	100.0	100.0

This supports those who claim rapid population growth results in these expenditures,[26] but the expenditure decisions for Western cities for the same categories would be inconsistent with this contention. Those cities spent markedly less on environmental protection in both 1973 (7.1 percent) and 1974 (7.0 percent) than cities in other regions. The street and road repair expenditures are more mixed, but offer little support for the regional growth theory.

Several other patterns are important. Northeastern cities allocated a sharply increased proportion of funds to health services in 1974 (6.5 percent) as compared to 1973 (1.4 percent). An interesting research topic would be to investigate the unionization effort of health service workers in the Northeast during this period. A similar pattern occurred in North Central cities regarding social services, which more than doubled from 2.0 percent in 1973 to 4.9 percent in 1974. Also note that Northeastern cities, perhaps reflecting the fiscal crisis they felt, were most likely to allocate their initial funds quickly (8.4 percent undetermined funds), while North Central (25.2 percent) and Western cities (24.3 percent) allocated their general revenue-sharing funds less rapidly. Since the differential in undetermined funds declined sharply in 1974, this may have been associated with the particular type of fiscal year in effect in the cities. Some cities operate on a July 1 to June 30 fiscal year; others have fiscal years corresponding with the calendar year; and still others have different beginning and ending dates for their fiscal years. Those with January 1 fiscal years may have been more likely to have allocated their initial funds than those with a July 1 fiscal year.

Finally, the expenditure pattern characterizing parks and recreation requires comment. Western cities allocated the largest proportion (11.5 percent and 19.1 percent each year), while Northeastern cities allocated the least (3.5 percent in 1973 and 5.5 percent in 1974). Southern cities allocated a sizeable proportion in both 1973 and 1974, while North Central cities did so in 1974. One possible explanation for the pattern is that Western and Southern cities may have had the opportunity to purchase significant park land and that increased public concern over parks and recreation provided the support necessary to justify the expenditure. Again, this would be a useful research hypothesis.

Tables 4-3 to 4-5 provide a series of useful comparisons, but do not, on the whole, offer much contrast to the expenditure patterns already discussed. General revenue-sharing expenditures tend to be concentrated in a few categories, and those categories have tended to gain a larger proportion of the 1974 general revenue-sharing funds than they did in 1973. It will be most interesting to see if these trends continue throughout the life of general revenue-sharing.[27]

Municipal Reform and Revenue Sharing Expenditures

As discussed in Chapter 1, one of the most interesting and often debated aspects of urban politics is the impact of structural variables on policy decisions. There has been and continues to be a lively interest in the interrelationships among such variables and the appropriate methodologies to investigate them.

Table 4-6 summarizes the general revenue sharing patterns for mayor-council and council-manager cities in 1973 and 1974. Table 4-6 indicates that there is indeed a different expenditure pattern associated with form of city government in 1974. Mayor-council cities spent decidedly more in both 1973 and 1974 on law enforcement and fire prevention than did council-manager cities. From 1973 to 1974, mayor-council cities increased their percentage of expenditures for these categories from 30.1 percent to 46.1 percent, while council-manager cities increased their expenditures for the same categories from 16.4 percent to 24.9 percent. Council-manager cities also spent nearly twice the percentage (15.0 percent to 7.9 percent) on the street and road repair categories as the mayor-council cities did in 1974. Council-manager cities also tended to allocate a larger percentage of revenue-sharing funds to parks and recreation expenditures in 1973 and 1974. The conclusion is clear; there is a different expenditure pattern when comparing government structure, but the direction and reason for that pattern is not apparent from the data in Table 4-6.

Appendix C summarizes a reform scale that was developed and used in our research. The reform scale, used in this and later chapters, ranges from 1 (least reformed) to 4 (most reformed). Assuming that reform and non-reform city governments behave differently and that this behavior may result in differing policy outcomes, a number of interesting hypotheses are possible. Certainly one of the more controversial ones is that reform cities will be more likely to expend a higher proportion of funds for services that have a greater tendency to benefit the entire population while the non-reform cities, due to more narrowly based political interests, will expend a higher proportion of funds for more geographically confined services.[28] Another possible relationship is that reform cities will be slower in allocating their funds because their decision-making process is more involved and has greater opportunity for increased planning and rationality prior to decision-making.[29] Table 4-7 summarizes the data necessary to investigate the hypotheses relating to structural reform.

Considering the 1973 data, there is evidence to support the three previously mentioned hypotheses. If park and recreation expenditures are taken as "community" expenditures and street and road repairs as "narrow" expenditures,[30] it is apparent that the structural variables did make a difference in 1973. Non-reform cities spent 20.8 percent of their initial funds for street and road repair, while reform cities spent less than half (9.4 percent) on the same item. Reform cities spent nearly twice as much (8.6 percent) on parks and recreation expenditures, than non-reform cities which spent 4.7 percent. Also, note that non-reform cities spent a considerably higher proportion of their general revenue-sharing funds on law enforcement (11 percent to 8.6 percent), fire prevention (14.3 percent to 5.6 percent) and environmental protection (16.4 percent to 12.5 percent) categories than did reform cities. Also, note that reform cities did in fact have more than twice the proportion (22.9 percent) of their funds undetermined as non-reform (8.4 percent) cities did. The 1973 results indicate substantial support for the structural theory and its impact on revenue-sharing decisions.

While the conclusions to be drawn from the 1974 results in Table 4-7 are not as consistent, they continue to support the contention that structural differences are indeed associated with expenditure differences. Reform cities spent twice the proportion (14.3 percent) of their funds on parks and recreation than did non-reform cities (6.3 percent). The reverse is true of the expected relationship for street and road repairs; reform cities spent nearly twice (13.9 percent) the proportion of funds than did non-reform cities (7.8 percent). This trend, if it persists, would cause hesitation concerning the applicability of the city-wide versus narrow benefits hypothesis.

Reform cities, although the proportion of undetermined funds in 1974 was drastically lower than in 1973 (5.6 percent to 22.9 percent), still had a larger proportion (5.6 percent to 2.1 percent) of undetermined funds than did non-reform cities. As was the case in 1973, reform cities spent a considerably smaller proportion of their funds on law enforcement (14.2 percent to 23.7 percent in 1974) and fire prevention (12.1 percent) to 24.1 percent in 1974) than did non-reform cities. This last point is particularly interesting.

Various authors have pointed out that non-reform cities are often dominated by political interests capable of strong organization and political knowledge.[31] Given the proportion of funds allocated to law enforcement and fire prevention categories, it would seem that police and fire organizations, as well as having a legitimate need for greater support, may have been more successful than other city employees or interest groups in gaining access to the local budgetary process and especially to the decision-making process as it relates to general revenue-sharing funds.

This success can be contrasted with that obtained by local citizen and community organizations wanting increased social and health expenditures. In these cases, relatively small proportions of revenue-sharing funds have gone to them. This is doubtlessly due to the previously mentioned points dealing with organization and political power.

Table 4-6
General Revenue-Sharing Expenditures and Form of Government

Expenditure Category	1973 Survey		1974 Survey	
	Mayor-Council (N = 74) %	Council-Manager (N = 126) %	Mayor-Council (N = 66) %	Council-Manager (N = 122) %
Law Enforcement	12.9	9.5	20.6	15.4
Fire Prevention	17.2	6.9	25.5	9.5
Building and Code Enforcement	1.0	1.1	.3	1.1
Environmental Protection	12.1	13.6	15.7	10.8
Transit Systems	3.1	1.2	1.5	3.6
Street and Road Repair	11.6	11.6	7.9	15.0
Social Services	2.0	1.4	3.5	2.7
Health	1.4	.9	2.4	2.2
Parks and Recreation	5.1	8.7	6.8	11.8
Building Renovation	3.1	4.5	.7	4.8
Libraries	1.8	3.8	.8	2.7
Municipal Salaries	4.5	1.2	.8	1.5
Other	13.8	12.0	11.1	13.7
Undertermined	10.4	23.6	2.4	5.2
Total	100.0	100.0	100.0	100.0

Table 4-7
General Revenue-Sharing Expenditures and Municipal Reformism

Expenditure Category	1973 Survey Municipal Reform				1974 Survey Municipal Reform			
	($N^1 = 24$) %	($N^2 = 45$) %	($N^3 = 39$) %	($N^4 = 93$) %	($N^1 = 28$) %	($N^2 = 41$) %	($N^3 = 33$) %	($N^4 = 95$) %
Law Enforcement	11.0	14.2	15.7	8.6	23.7	17.6	13.7	14.2
Fire Prevention	14.3	17.9	10.4	5.6	24.1	21.6	7.8	12.1
Building and Code Enforcement	.2	.2	2.4	1.5	.3	.8	.4	.9
Environmental Protection	16.4	13.3	10.9	12.5	12.5	17.5	13.9	11.0
Transit Systems	1.4	2.2	3.1	1.5	1.2	3.0	5.3	2.8
Street and Road Repair	20.8	8.3	15.0	9.4	7.8	10.2	18.2	13.9
Social Services	1.4	2.4	1.9	1.4	2.8	1.0	6.0	2.9
Health	1.9	1.3	1.0	1.1	3.9	2.3	3.5	1.7
Parks and Recreation	4.7	4.5	9.8	8.6	6.3	10.5	6.2	14.3
Building Renovation	5.9	1.4	2.3	5.6	1.5	1.6	5.0	4.2
Libraries	.8	.6	2.3	1.5	1.4	.9	.7	3.5
Municipal Salaries	1.1	4.4	5.9	4.5	-0-	1.9	2.9	.6
Other	11.7	19.0	1.8	15.3	12.4	7.9	13.4	12.3
Undetermined	8.4	10.3	17.5	22.9	2.1	3.2	3.0	5.6
Total	100.0	100.0	100.0	100.0	100.0	100.0	100.0	100.0

In sum, then, expenditure decisions are indeed associated with governmental structure and at least the two extremes of the reform index and except in one case, in the expected direction. The fact that there is no clear tendency for expenditure decisions to be consistent throughout the four index categories indicates that the middle scores (2 and 3) may require additional refinement and consideration.

Revenue-Sharing Decisions and Demographic Variables

As previously discussed, those interested in policy research have developed and used a number of demographic variables that attempt to measure the impact population composition, socioeconomic characteristics, and population change have on policy outcomes.[32] For our purposes, three variables were chosen to represent the major demographic characteristics.

Mean income was selected as the variable to measure an individual city's relative socioeconomic standing.[33] While other variables also do this, it was felt that this single variable most accurately and completely reflects overall economic strength. Expenditure patterns could be expected to be different as mean income varies;[34] a variety of hypothesis are possible. For instance, one could argue that low-income cities will allocate larger proportions of their budgets to social and health services as well as building renovation, while more affluent cities will be more likely to spend their money on parks and recreation, libraries, and other services that more indirectly benefit the recipient.

Table 4-8 summarizes the expenditure patterns for the cities when they are divided into three categories: those with mean incomes under $10,500; those between $10,500 and $12,500; and those over $12,500. As the table indicates, cities did not appear to differentiate spending decisions as their mean income increased—at least not in the expected way. Cities, regardless of income level, tended to allocate similar proportions of general revenue-sharing funds to law enforcement activities in 1973 and 1974 as well as to fire prevention in 1974. There is an inconsistent and slight deviation in the 1973 expenditures for fire prevention.

Considering the earlier hypotheses, the evidence is inconclusive. In 1973, higher-income cities spent a smaller proportion of their revenue-sharing funds (4.7 percent) for parks and recreation than did low- (6.8 percent) and middle-income (8.8 percent) cities; however in 1974, the wealthier cities spent the highest proportion (13.4 percent) on parks and recreation. Note the similar proportions spent by the cities in the various categories on building and code enforcement and building renovation in 1973 and 1974. This does not support the contention that city income has a marked impact on expenditure patterns.

Table 4-8
Mean Income and General Revenue-Sharing Expenditures

Expenditure Category	1973 Survey (N = 213)			1974 Survey (N = 216)		
	Less than $10,500 (N = 73)	$10,500 to $12,500 (N = 93)	Over $12,500 (N = 47)	Less than $10,500 (N = 82)	$10,500 to $12,500 (N = 84)	Over $12,500 (N = 50)
Law Enforcement	11.0	12.1	10.1	15.3	16.7	17.3
Fire Prevention	9.8	12.1	7.4	16.5	15.3	13.3
Building and Code Enforcement	1.5	1.8	.5	.3	1.0	.9
Environmental Protection	13.6	9.8	16.7	14.0	10.4	16.6
Transit Systems	2.2	1.8	1.4	2.9	3.5	2.2
Street and Road Repair	13.2	12.3	7.5	12.0	15.4	8.6
Social Services	2.1	1.0	2.2	1.8	2.7	4.7
Health	2.6	1.0	.9	3.6	1.7	3.5
Parks and Recreation	6.8	8.8	4.7	10.4	11.1	13.4
Building Renovation	4.2	3.6	4.5	3.5	4.2	3.9
Libraries	1.4	1.8	.4	1.5	1.3	4.6
Municipal Salaries	5.5	3.0	4.8	1.0	1.1	.5
Other	14.9	5.7	20.1	11.7	13.6	7.3
Undetermined	11.2	25.2	18.8	5.5	3.0	3.2
Total	100.0	100.0	100.0	100.0	100.0	100.0

Even more damaging to this contention are the health and social services categories. In 1973, the relationship for health services expenditures is as expected—that is, inversely related to increasing income—but this is not the case for 1974. Social services received its largest proportion of funds in the wealthier cities in both 1973 (2.2 percent) and 1974 (4.7 percent), while the proportion allocated to social services in 1974 in low-income cities (1.8 percent) actually declined over 1973 (2.1 percent) totals. One possible explanation is that wealthier cities may not qualify for other federal programs and decided to use revenue-sharing funds to provide these services, while the lower-income cities either already had such programs or had too many other demands on their revenue-sharing funds. Whatever the reasons, economic affluence, measured by mean income, did not result in highly differentiated expenditure patterns.

Another variable often used in policy research is that measuring the proportion of non-white population.[35] The assumption is that cities with different racial composition will have the needs of the differing racial groups reflected in expenditure patterns.[36] For instance, one expected relationship would be that cities with greater non-white percentages would be more likely to spend a higher proportion of funds on social and health services and less on environmental protection due to the more pressing needs in the former areas. Table 4-9 summarizes the expenditure patterns for the responding cities according to the percent non-white population. As was the case with income, city expenditure patterns do not vary as expected when compared on the basis of a city's non-white percentage.

In 1973, the 65 cities with non-white population over 15 percent actually spent the lowest proportion of their funds for both social (1 percent) and health (.9 percent) services. In 1974, a similar pattern is evident. In 1973, the expected relationship regarding environmental protection does indeed appear to hold as the proportion expended declines as non-white percentage increases, but this is not the case in 1974 when cities over 15 percent and under 5 percent non-white allocated quite similar proportions (13.3 percent and 14.2 percent) for environmental protection.

Perhaps the most interesting aspect of Table 4-9 is the similarity in the amounts expended for law enforcement and fire prevention regardless of percent non-white. The proportion allocated to both categories by all the various cities increased from 1973 to 1974 and the increase was relatively constant. It would be wrong to reach far-reaching conclusions based on this trend, but it does tend to support the contention that non-white groups need and indeed want increased law enforcement and fire prevention services in their areas of the cities. It would be most interesting to investigate the distribution of revenue-sharing funds within the various neighborhoods and to the population groups located in the city. Unfortunately data on

Table 4-9
Non-White Population and General Revenue-Sharing Expenditures

Expenditure Category	1973 Survey (N = 212)			1974 Survey (N = 215)		
	Less than 5% (N = 92)	5% to 15% (N = 55)	Over 15% (N = 65)	Less than 5% (N = 99)	5% to 15% (N = 53)	Over 15% (N = 63)
Law Enforcement	11.6	10.9	11.0	15.8	17.7	15.8
Fire Prevention	8.2	12.6	11.5	14.9	13.9	17.2
Building and Code Enforcement	2.2	1.3	.6	.2	1.6	.8
Environmental Protection	14.1	13.0	9.9	14.2	11.3	13.3
Transit Systems	1.9	.7	2.6	2.6	3.2	3.1
Street and Road Repair	10.8	14.3	10.4	12.5	11.7	13.4
Social Services	2.0	2.1	1.0	2.6	3.2	2.6
Health	2.1	1.3	.9	3.2	2.4	2.8
Parks and Recreation	8.7	5.6	6.2	13.4	8.1	9.0
Building Renovation	5.1	2.9	3.3	3.4	5.1	3.5
Libraries	2.1	1.3	.5	2.1	3.0	1.4
Municipal Salaries	3.5	1.8	7.5	.3	1.1	2.3
Other	10.6	9.9	15.5	10.6	14.7	10.4
Undetermined	17.1	22.3	19.1	4.2	3.0	4.4
Total	100.0	100.0	100.0	100.0	100.0	100.0

these distributions are extremely difficult to obtain, but such data would be required if one wished to satisfactorily pursue this point.

The final demographic variable used in the analysis is the percentage population change encountered by cities from 1960 to 1970. Investigators have often utilized a population change variable,[37] but it is becoming increasingly utilized with the awareness that American cities are experiencing widely differentiating growth rates with Southern and Western cities growing rapidly, while North Central and Northeastern cities have better relatively stable populations or have been losing population. Table 4-10 divides the responding cities into three categories based on population change (cities that lost population, those that remained stable or gained up to 25 percent, and those that gained over 25 percent from 1960 to 1970) and summarizes the revenue-sharing decisions reached by cities in each category.

Population growth does appear to have an impact on expenditure decisions as the following examples illustrate. With one exception (police expenditures in 1974 for cities with over a 25 percent growth rate), the proportion of revenue-sharing funds allocated to law enforcement and fire prevention declined the more rapidly the city was growing. Also, note the large percentage allocated to these two categories in 1974 (23.8 percent and 26.7 percent respectively) by those cities that lost population from 1960 to 1970. This is similar to the pattern associated with regional differences and is no doubt strongly correlated. What appears to happen is that cities in the Northeast that are losing population spend a far larger proportion of their general revenue-sharing funds on law enforcement and fire prevention. Again question of political organization of benefiting groups is raised as well as the needs of these cities to provide basic services.

The law enforcement and fire prevention categories are not the only expenditure items that support the contention that population growth is markedly related to expenditure decisions. Parks and recreation proportional expenditures are also consistent in that these expenditures received a larger proportion of general revenue-sharing funds in both 1973 and 1974 as population growth increased. Interestingly, the proportions allocated for building and code enforcement and building renovation (with several exceptions) tended to increase as population growth increased.

Despite these supporting findings, there is some conflicting evidence. For instance, the proportion allocated for environmental protection does not increase as population change increases and the pattern for street and road repair expenditures is inconsistent. Also, no clear pattern develops in the social and health services categories. While these exceptions should be noted, they do not negate the general conclusions that revenue-sharing decisions in 1973 and 1974 were associated with different population growth rates.

Table 4-10
Population Change and Revenue-Sharing Expenditures

Expenditure Category	1973 Survey (N = 213) Population Change			1974 Survey (N = 216) Population Change		
	Less than 0% (N = 58)	0% to 25% (N = 92)	More than 25% (N = 63)	Less than 0% (N = 58)	0% to 25% (N = 105)	More than 25% (N = 53)
Law Enforcement	13.7	11.0	9.6	23.8	13.4	14.0
Fire Prevention	13.7	9.7	7.9	26.7	11.8	9.8
Building and Code Enforcement	.7	.4	3.6	.8	.4	1.3
Environmental Protection	7.7	14.9	13.9	10.7	15.6	11.2
Transit Systems	2.0	1.2	2.7	2.1	4.2	2.0
Street and Road Repair	12.5	9.3	14.0	12.4	10.1	17.6
Social Services	1.4	1.2	2.8	3.0	2.5	3.1
Health	2.2	.6	2.2	2.3	3.6	1.7
Parks and Recreation	4.0	7.3	10.1	4.3	12.3	15.4
Building Renovation	4.1	1.7	7.2	1.7	4.2	5.5
Libraries	1.4	.8	2.2	1.6	2.2	2.7
Municipal Salaries	7.4	1.9	4.7	—	2.0	.5
Other	15.1	17.6	.7	8.7	13.6	9.1
Undetermined	14.1	22.4	18.4	1.9	4.1	6.1
Total	100.0	100.0	100.0	100.0	100.0	100.0

Conclusion

Careful consideration of the various tables as well as the complex data summarized in this chapter clearly indicates the following points.

First, revenue-sharing expenditures have been concentrated in the law enforcement, fire prevention, environmental protection, street and road repair, and parks and recreation categories. It appears that the proportion of funds allocated to these five categories is increasing and that in cities over 50,000 the aggregate total expended accounts for nearly 70 percent of the total general revenue-sharing funds available.

Second, social and health services programs have not received large proportions of general revenue-sharing funds, but social services have received a larger proportion of general revenue-sharing funds than they had in prior budgetary years.

Third, of the structural variables investigated, size was associated with increasing proportion of funds for law enforcement and fire prevention, city type did not have much influence on expenditure decisions, and regional location resulted in a variety of interesting and important expenditure patterns.

Fourth, governmental structures were found to be associated with differing revenue-sharing expenditure patterns. Mayor-council cities tended to spend a higher percentage on law enforcement and fire protection, while council-manager cities spent a higher percentage on parks and recreation expenditures. The same pattern was generally found when a reform scale was used to characterize cities. This supports those who contend the effect(s) that differing political structures have on policy outcomes.

Fifth, of the demographic variables investigated, only population growth had a marked and consistent impact on the revenue-sharing expenditure patterns. Non-white population and mean income were not associated with widely differing expenditure patterns among the cities.

Throughout the chapter, possible hypotheses and explanations have been developed and considered. A point that has been alluded to and will be more fully discussed in the next chapters is the responsiveness of city governments to the various political and citizen demands made upon them.[38] While aggregate expenditure patterns permit generalized conclusions, it is difficult to draw basic conclusions about the political process and causal nature of policy making. The next chapter develops these points.

Notes

1. Intergovernmental Relations Subcommittee of the Committee on

Government Operations, House of Representatives, *Replies by Members of Congress to a Questionnaire on General Revenue Sharing* (Washington, D.C.: Government Printing Office, 1974), p. v.

2. Henry S. Reuss, *Revenue Sharing* (New York: Praeger, 1970), pp. 71-80.

3. For provisions of the general revenue-sharing legislation see Public Law 92-512. For a brief and uncomplicated summary of the legislation see, *What Is General Revenue Sharing* (Washington, D.C.: Office of Revenue Sharing, 1973).

4. *Replies by Members of Congress to a Questionnaire on General Revenue Sharing,* p.v.

5. For a summary of the research in progress in December 1973, see *Compendium of Research in Progress* (Washington, D.C.: National Planning Association, 1973).

6. For descriptions of the Brookings research, see *Compendium of Research in Progress,* p. 18.

7. Ibid.

8. For a description of this project see *Compendium of Research in Progress,* pp. 19-20.

9. This data obtained from Table 5 of U.S. Bureau of the Census, *City Government Finances in 1970-1971* (Washington, D.C.: Government Printing Office, 1972).

10. This data was obtained from the *Municipal Year Book* (Washington, D.C.: International City Management Association, 1968).

11. This data was obtained from a variety of 1970 census publications.

12. See *Replies of Members of Congress to a Questionnaire on General Revenue Sharing,* pp. 6-10.

13. For a discussion of budgeting in general, see Aaron Wildavsky, *The Politics of the Budgetary Process* (Boston: Little, Brown and Co., 1964). For a detailed discussion of municipal budgeting in three large cities, see John P. Crecine, *Government Problem-Solving* (Chicago: Rand McNally, 1969). For a differing interpretation of municipal budgeting in medium size cities, see David A. Caputo, "The Normative and Empirical Implication of the Budgetary Processes of Four Medium-Size Cities," (unpublished Ph.D. dissertation, Yale University, 1970).

14. For information on municipal unionism, see David T. Stanley, *Managing Local Government Under Union Pressure* (Washington: Brookings Institution, 1972), and Jack Stieber, "Employee Representation in Municipal Government," *The Municipal Year Book* (Washington: International City Management Association, 1969), pp. 31-57.

15. As an example see the Office of Revenue Sharing's publication *Getting Involved: Your Guide to General Revenue Sharing* (March, 1974).

16. See *Replies of Members of Congress to a Questionnaire on General Revenue Sharing,* pp. 6-7, for such statements.

17. We realize that the analysis of general revenue-sharing decision making is just beginning but feel the variables we have chosen reflect prior research in other budgetary areas. Of course, other variables will and should be investigated.

18. For summary articles, see Robert L. Lineberry and Edmund P. Fowler, "Reformism and Public Policies in American Cities," *The American Political Science Review* LXI (September, 1967), pp. 701-716; and Richard L. Cole, "The Urban Policy Process: A Note on Structural and Regional Influences," *Social Science Quarterly* (December 1971), pp. 648-656.

19. Robert C. Wood, *1400 Governments* (Garden City, N.Y.: Doubleday Anchor Books, 1961), p. 31.

20. Keep in mind that cities were faced with mounting demands for services while having a restricted amount of resources available.

21. For instance, see Robert C. Wood, *Suburbia.* (Boston: Houghton Mifflin, 1958).

22. Amos H. Hawley, "Metropolitan Population and Municipal Government Expenditures in Central Cities," *Journal of Social Issues* (January-March 1951), pp. 100-8.

23. See Brett W. Hawkins, *Politics and Urban Policies* (Indianapolis: Bobbs-Merrill Company, 1971), Chapter 2, "The Environmental Base of Urban Governmental Forms," pp. 19-59.

24. For a particularly interesting discussion on this point, see Richard D. Feld, "The Impact of Population Growth on Public Policy Formulation in Rapidly Growing Urban Areas of the United States" in Virginia Gray and Elihu Bergman (eds.), *Political Issues in United States Population Policy* (Lexington, Mass.: D.C. Heath, Lexington Books, 1974).

25. Stanley, pp. 10-14.

26. Feld, "The Impact of Population . . ."

27. We plan to continue our research through at least 1976. By having satisfactory base data, we should be able to monitor and evaluate trends as they develop and continue. In addition, our data will provide an interesting comparative basis for official reports and documents dealing with general revenue-sharing expenditures.

28. See James Q. Wilson and Edward C. Banfield, "Political Ethos Revisited," *The American Political Science Review* LXV (December, 1971), pp. 1050-6 for a discussion of the point.

29. Ibid.

30. Ibid.

31. An excellent example is Robert Dahl's, *Who Governs?* (New Haven: Yale University Press, 1961).

32. See Lineberry and Fowler, p. 703 and Hawkins, pp. 61-84.

33. The individual city's mean income was obtained from Table 89 of the 1970 Census.

34. Harvey E. Brazer, *City Expenditures in the United States* (New York: National Bureau of Economic Research Incorporated, 1959), pp. 29, 65-68.

35. See Lineberry and Fowler, p. 703.

36. For an interesting consideration of the impact of general revenue sharing on non-white populations, see *The Minority Community and Revenue Sharing* (Washington: The Joint Center for Political Studies, 1973).

37. See Richard D. Feld, "The Impact of Population Growth . . ." for a discussion of this point.

38. For an interesting discussion of responsiveness see, Lineberry and Fowler, pp. 715-6. This point will be discussed in later chapters.

Program Consequences of General Revenue Sharing: Policy Innovation, Citizen Participation, and Taxing Efforts

Introduction

Beyond its direct fiscal implications, general revenue sharing is likely to have significant consequences for American cities in a number of program and policy areas. These include such critical issues as the degree to which general revenue sharing has facilitated policy innovation at the local level; the extent to which citizen input has been encouraged in the expenditure of revenue-sharing funds and the impact of such participation; the effect of revenue sharing on categorical grant programs and the taxing efforts of recipient governments; and the attitudes of local officials toward the general revenue-sharing program. These issues are addressed in this chapter.

Revenue Sharing and Program Innovation

The degree to which general revenue sharing has encouraged the development of new and innovative programs at the municipal level is of interest to those concerned specifically with the revenue-sharing legislation as well as to urban scholars in general. Those who have closely followed the revenue-sharing legislation have expressed hope, at least, that this new source of funds would lead to new and creative urban programs. However, many have found that the funds are being used mainly to support on-going programs and services. An article appearing in the February 21, 1973 issue of the *New York Times,* for example, found that, as a whole, cities and states have been reluctant to expend revenue-sharing funds for new social programs. Although the article admits that information is fragmentary, it goes on to conclude that most state and local officials regard revenue sharing as a windfall and allocate the funds accordingly.[1]

Of course, the basic philosophy of revenue sharing is that expenditure decisions should be made at the local level, according to local needs, and it would be unfair to conclude that the measure is less than a success if all or most of the funds are used primarily to supplement existing programs. Yet, it is clear that one of the primary arguments of the Nixon Administration in support of revenue sharing was that it would facilitate the implementation of new programs and services at the local level. President Nixon, himself, in his 1971 State of the Union Address, stated that previous grant programs often treated state and local officials "as children who are given a meager allowance, told precisely how to spend it, and then are scolded for not being self-reliant enough to handle [it] more responsibly." By "putting more power in more places," the former president predicted in that address that "we can make the government more creative in more places."[2] Also, in his 1972 State of the Union Address, President Nixon again stressed the theme that revenue sharing would encourage program innovation at the local level. In that speech, he stated, "Revenue sharing can bring a new sense of accountability, a new burst of energy and a new spirit of creativity to our federal system."[3] In addition, the easing of the financial "crisis" faced by American cities in the late 1960s has led many to assume that revenue-sharing funds could be used for program innovation.[4]

The issue of innovation in the use of public funds is of interest beyond its specific application to revenue-sharing grants. In fact, very little presently is known about those political and environmental factors associated with policy innovation at the municipal level. Much of the literature would suggest that more centralized political structures—such as that found in the city manager form of government, non-partisan politics, and at large elections—would facilitate policy innovation;[5] however, the most comprehensive empirical examination of policy innovation at the local level has found that cities with these political structures are *less* likely to be innovative in the public policy arena.[6] The allocation of revenue-sharing funds provides an additional opportunity to examine innovation at the local level.

The survey conducted for this study asked the respondents to indicate, in general, whether the majority of revenue-sharing money was used to fund new or on-going programs. Table 5-1 presents their replies.

It is apparent that most cities applied most of their revenue-sharing funds to existing programs rather than to new activities. As is indicated in Table 5-1, only 29 percent of the cities reported spending most of their funds primarily on new programs. An analysis of the spending patterns by form of government indicates some interesting deviations in this overall trend. Manager forms of government and those considered to be the most "reformed"[7] were most likely to spend their funds in new program areas. Thus, these findings would lend some credence to the assumption that reformed political structures facilitate policy innovation. At the same time, it is true that reform political structures tend to be associated with demographic and environmental factors,[8] and it is possible that the patterns noted in Table 5-1 are more a function of these factors than of political variables. Table 5-2 examines innovation in the use of revenue sharing by these various demographic factors.

As Table 5-2 demonstrates, the expenditure of revenue-sharing funds on new programs appears to be markedly related to a number of environmental factors. Smaller, suburban cities in the South and West are more

Table 5-1
Use of Revenue Sharing for New and Existing Programs, by Form of Government

| | Revenue Sharing Used Mainly for | | | |
	Existing Programs		New Programs	
Total, All Cities[a]	71.0% (137)		29.0% (56)	
Form of Government				
Mayor	80.0	(52)	20.0	(13)
Manager	65.0	(76)	35.0	(41)
Municipal Reform[b]				
1	78.3	(18)	21.7	(5)
2	78.0	(32)	22.0	(9)
3	69.7	(23)	30.3	(10)
4	64.0	(55)	36.0	(31)

[a]In this and the following tables, subtotal frequencies may not equal summary totals because of missing data for a few cities.
[b]The measure of municipal "reformism" used in this study is explained in Appendix C.
Note: Data used in this table were derived from the 1973 survey.

likely to allocate their revenue-sharing funds to new program areas as are cities with greater wealth and with lower proportions of non-white population. Thus, it can be concluded that policy innovation, as measured by this survey, is at least as much a factor of environmental criteria as political factors. The straightforward conclusion appears to be that those cities experiencing greater social and fiscal problems were less able to channel revenue-sharing dollars into new programs and services. Instead, they found it necessary to use these funds to maintain and bolster on-going programs. It might also be inferred from these data that as the fiscal crises in larger, central cities subside,[9] more cities will allocate larger proportions of their revenue-sharing grants to new and innovative programs.

It is also of interest to examine the innovative use of revenue-sharing funds by policy area. Although the overall trend by municipalities has been to spend revenue-sharing funds for on-going programs, this pattern may be altered when examining specific policy areas. Table 5-3 presents this information.

As indicated in Table 5-3, some very interesting variations in the overall trend of cities to spend their revenue-sharing funds on existing programs is evident. It is found that in functional categories such as transit systems, social services, parks and recreation, and libraries, cities spend a substantial proportion of their revenue-sharing funds in new program areas. Thus, the overall conclusion of this section is that, as many have speculated, the

Table 5-2
Use of Revenue-Sharing for New and Existing Programs by Environmental Factors

| | Revenue Sharing Used Mainly For | | | |
	Existing Programs		New Programs	
Total, All Cities	71.0%	(137)	29.0%	(56)
City Size				
50,000 to 100,000	68.7	(79)	31.3	(36)
100,000 to 250,000	62.7	(32)	37.3	(19)
250,000 to 500,000	94.1	(16)	5.9	(1)
Over 500,000	100.0	(10)	0.0	(0)
City Type				
Central	76.2	(93)	23.8	(29)
Suburban	62.0	(44)	38.0	(27)
Region				
Northeast	73.7	(28)	26.3	(10)
North Central	79.6	(39)	20.4	(10)
South	66.7	(38)	33.3	(19)
West	65.3	(32)	34.7	(17)
Mean Income				
Less than $10,500	77.9	(53)	22.1	(15)
$10,500 to $12,500	71.4	(60)	28.6	(24)
Over $12,500	58.5	(24)	41.5	(17)
Proportion Non-White				
Less than 5.0%	63.4	(52)	36.6	(30)
5.0 to 15.0%	76.5	(39)	23.5	(12)
Over 15.0%	76.7	(46)	23.3	(14)
Population Change				
Less than 0.0%	72.7	(40)	27.3	(15)
0.0 to 25.0%	76.8	(63)	23.2	(19)
Over 25.0%	60.7	(34)	39.3	(22)

Note: Data used in this table derived from the 1973 survey.

majority of cities spend most of their revenue-sharing funds in existing and on-going service areas; however, this is modified to the extent that wealthier, smaller suburban cities were more likely to allocate their funds to new services and some categories of spending were more likely to have been for new services than were others.

Citizen Participation and the Allocation of Revenue-Sharing Funds

An extremely interesting aspect of the allocation of revenue-sharing funds concerns the degree to which citizen participation in those allocation

Table 5-3
Use of Revenue Sharing for New and Existing Programs, by Function

Function:	Revenue Sharing Used for[a]		
	Existing Programs	Both Equally	New Programs
Law Enforcement	76.4%	4.7%	18.9%
Fire Prevention	82.3	5.3	12.4
Building and Code Enforcement	76.7	0.0	23.3
Environmental Protection	69.1	6.4	24.5
Transit Systems	60.9	8.7	30.4
Street and Road Repair	76.1	8.0	15.9
Social Services	45.8	6.8	47.4
Health	66.7	7.4	25.9
Parks and Recreation	55.6	6.5	37.9
Building Renovation	71.1	0.0	28.9
Libraries	62.0	6.0	32.0
Financial Administration	66.7	7.0	26.3
Other	51.7	5.0	43.3

[a]It should be noted that our questions on innovation differed in our two surveys. In 1973, we asked the single question, "Would you say that revenue-sharing funds received to date by your city have been used (or will be used) mainly to supplement, improve, or extend existing services or have they been used (or will be used) mainly to fund *new* programs?" In 1974, we asked respondents to indicate for each expenditure category whether the funds had been used primarily for new or existing programs. Table 5-3 represents responses to our 1974 question; Tables 5-1 and 5-2 are based on the 1973 question. See Appendix A for a listing of the questions utilized.

Note: This table based on 1974 survey data. Functions not listed were too seldomly selected for meaningful comparisons.

decisions has been encouraged (or tolerated). One of the distinguishing characteristics of general revenue sharing, as compared with previous major urban-oriented programs, such as those funded by OEO and Model Cities, is that revenue sharing requires no participation of citizens in the allocation of funds. Rather, decisions concerning the allocation of revenue-sharing money are left entirely to the recipient government.[10] A number of observers have been severely critical of this aspect of general revenue sharing. For example, as recently as May 1974, Reverend Jesse Jackson noted: "There are still no provisions for citizens to petition the preliminary use of revenue-sharing funds. Nor are there adequate provisions in the regulations permitting citizen input for the planning phase of fund use. It is questionable to allow . . . units of local government to utilize freely some $30 billion over a five-year period without qualified citizens' audit."[11]

It is clear that even in the absence of provisions requiring such involvement, a number of cities accepted President Nixon's challenge that revenue sharing should "send power . . . back to the people"[12] and have invited citizen involvement in their spending decisions. Gary Mayor Richard

Table 5-4
Public Hearings and the Allocation of Revenue-Sharing Funds

| | Public Hearings Held Prior to This Year's Allocation? | | Public Hearings to be Held in the Future? | | |
	Yes	No	Yes	No	Undecided
1973	49.7%	50.3%	37.7%	37.7%	24.6%
(n)	(97)	(98)	(75)	(75)	(49)
1974	58.6%	41.4%	50.7%	49.3%	—[a]
(n)	(119)	(84)	(104)	(101)	

[a]This option was not provided in the 1974 survey.

Hatcher, commenting on the degree of citizen participation in revenue-sharing decisions in his city, stated: "That is one aspect of revenue sharing of which we are justifiably proud. Each time we allocated revenue-sharing funds, we urged citizens to add any recommendations or suggestions . . . we extensively advertised a public hearing . . . we invited anyone and everyone in the community to present proposals. . . . At that hearing, the turnout was excellent."[13] Although the degree of participation as described in Gary undoubtedly is not typical of citizen participation in other cities, Table 5-4 indicates that almost half of all the officials responding to this survey did indicate that their cities had held public hearings prior to their decisions on revenue sharing.

Interestingly, Table 5-4 indicates an increase from 1973 to 1974 (49.7 percent to 58.6 percent) in the tendency of cities to hold public hearings prior to the expenditure of revenue-sharing funds. Also, the table indicates a notable increase in the proportion of cities indicating that public hearings concerning the allocation of revenue-sharing funds are to be held in the future. Thus, it is found that although the revenue-sharing legislation requires no citizen input, almost half of the officials responding to this survey indicated that their cities had held public hearings in 1973 and almost 60 percent indicated that their cities held such hearings in 1974. Although no formal citizen participation is required, it is clear that the revenue-sharing legislation has elicited considerable citizen input. Table 5-5 examines this participation while "controlling for" various environmental and political factors.

Overall, Table 5-5 conforms relatively well to participation patterns noted in previous studies. Others have found that larger, central cities are more likely to encourage participation in any form,[14] and this is true concerning revenue sharing as well as indicated by the proportion of cities over 500,000 holding public hearings. Perhaps the major exception to what might have been expected concerns the fact that council-manager cities were somewhat more likely to have held public hearings than were mayor-

Table 5-5
Public Hearings and the Allocation of Revenue-Sharing by Political, En-vironmental and Demographic Characteristics

	Holding Public Hearings		Not Holding Public Hearings	
Total, All Cities	58.6%	(119)	41.4%	(84)
Form of Government				
Mayor	53.3	(32)	46.7	(28)
Manager	61.5	(72)	38.5	(45)
Municipal Reform[a]				
1	62.5	(15)	37.5	(9)
2	52.6	(20)	47.4	(18)
3	61.3	(19)	38.7	(12)
4	62.6	(57)	37.4	(34)
City Size				
50,000 to 100,000	52.2	(60)	47.8	(55)
100,000 to 250,000	71.4	(40)	28.6	(16)
250,000 to 500,000	52.4	(11)	47.6	(10)
Over 500,000	72.7	(8)	27.3	(3)
City Type				
Central	65.1	(82)	34.9	(44)
Suburban	46.4	(32)	53.6	(37)
Region				
Northeast	41.9	(18)	58.1	(25)
North Central	53.6	(30)	46.4	(26)
South	74.5	(35)	25.5	(12)
West	63.3	(31)	36.7	(18)
Mean Income				
Less than $10,500	58.4	(45)	41.6	(32)
$10,500 to $12,500	61.5	(48)	38.5	(30)
Over $12,500	54.2	(26)	45.8	(22)
Proportion Non-White				
Less than 5.0%	48.9	(46)	51.1	(48)
5.0 to 15.0%	65.4	(34)	34.6	(18)
Over 15.0%	68.4	(39)	31.6	(18)
Population Change				
Less than 0.0%	50.0	(27)	50.0	(27)
0.0 to 25.0%	61.2	(60)	38.8	(38)
Over 25.0%	62.7	(32)	37.3	(19)

[a]The measure of municipal "reformism" used in this study is explained in Appendix C.
Note: Data in this table are based on the 1974 survey.

council cities. This is precisely opposite what would be expected given the supposed "professional" biases of council-manager cities.[15] It might be concluded that mayor-council cities are more concerned with encouraging an involved citizenry in decision-making and then being subject to political reprisal if the public's suggestions are not followed. Alternately, one might

Table 5-6
Effect of Public Hearings on Revenue-Sharing Allocations

Function	Cities Holding Public Hearings		Cities Not Holding Public Hearings	
	1973 (%)	1974 (%)	1973 (%)	1974 (%)
Environmental Protection	11.7	13.0	12.8	13.6
Law Enforcement	11.1	12.2	12.8	22.7
Street and Road Repair	10.3	15.4	12.3	9.2
Fire Prevention	11.2	13.4	10.4	17.4
Parks and Recreation	9.4	12.6	5.7	7.2
Building Renovation	4.1	4.1	3.7	3.9
Salaries	2.5	.6	5.3	1.3
Direct Tax Relief	.6	1.1	2.2	.2
Transit Systems	1.1	3.5	2.0	2.3
Social Services	1.9	3.9	.6	1.7
Debt Retirement	1.4	.2	1.3	.7
Health	1.5	3.8	.9	1.6
Libraries	1.0	1.4	1.3	3.2
Building Code Enforcement	1.7	.6	.1	.8
Investments	.1	.5	.3	—
Financial Administration	—	1.6	—	1.0
Other	9.8	8.3	11.4	8.2
Undetermined	20.6	3.8	16.9	5.0

conclude that citizens felt their channels to decision-making were more open in mayor-council cities and that the need for public hearings in these cities was less than in manager cities.[16] In any case, it is clear that council-manager cities were somewhat more likely to have citizen input in the allocation of revenue-sharing funds than were mayor-council cities.

Also, it is important to examine the degree to which citizen input appears to have made a difference in the allocation of revenue-sharing funds. Obviously, the decision to hold or not to hold public hearings is of little objective utility (beyond whatever psychological or cathartic benefits may accrue to the participants), unless such citizen participation in fact has an impact on the content of decisions. Table 5-6 explores this question.

Table 5-6 presents some very interesting deviations from the overall spending patterns reported in Chapter 4. Cities that did *not* hold public hearings were much more likely to allocate their revenue-sharing funds for public safety functions. Although these deviations were slight in 1973, they were quite noticeable in 1974 when cities not holding public hearings spent over 40 percent of their general revenue-sharing funds for law enforcement and fire prevention, compared with about 26 percent spent for these functions by cities that did hold public hearings.

Cities that did hold public hearings, on the other hand, were more likely to evenly distribute their funds (although they also allocated a substantial proportion to public safety functions) and spent larger proportions of their money in such areas as street and road repair (in 1974) parks and recreation, direct tax relief, social services, and health services. The implications of these findings, we believe, are very significant. As noted in Chapter 1, traditional theories of American federalism would argue that as the locus of decision-making shifts from the national to the local level, decisions that are more status-quo-oriented are more likely to result. Certainly this study finds, as these theories would predict, that large proportions of general revenue-sharing funds are being spent on items reflecting this. At the same time, again as suggested in Chapter 1, increased organization and politicization of previously politically inactive or powerless groups may affect subsequent expenditure decisions. The findings in Table 5-6 indicate that cities having groups of citizens participate in general revenue-sharing expenditure decisions do appear to spend their funds in a more redistributive fashion (i.e., less money for public safety functions and more for social services, health, and other amenities). While the differences, in most cases, are relatively slight, a pattern has developed that suggests citizen organization and participation may reverse the predicted results of decentralized decision making. Of course, it should be noted that aggregate data such as that presented in Table 5-6 do not "prove" a causal relationship between citizen participation and the expenditure of revenue-sharing funds. Other factors, such as city size, mean income, and racial composition, may also affect these decisions, as discussed in Chapter 4. Nevertheless, it is significant that cities that had citizen input did noticeably differ in their expenditure of general revenue-sharing funds, and the data presented here would suggest that such participation may have been an important factor in this difference. This would be an extremely interesting area for future research to pursue.

Impact of Revenue Sharing on Categorical Grant Programs and Municipal Taxing Levels

Two of the most often discussed aspects of the general revenue-sharing legislation are its implications for municipal programs currently being funded by categorical grant sources (such as OEO and Model Cities) and its impact on municipal taxing rates. The data collected for this study provide some interesting insights in these two areas.

A particularly sensitive area concerns the impact of the revenue-sharing concept on programs such as Community Action Agencies and Model Cities activities. Although former President Nixon publicly stated that there was little reason to believe that revenue-sharing would mean a dismantlement of these programs,[17] there are those who fear that revenue-sharing funds are meant to be a substitute for—and eventually will lead to a phasing out of—those activities supported by Model Cities and OEO legislation. Senators Gaylord Nelson and Jacob Javits are among those very much concerned about the future of community action programs and have sponsored legislation that would provide money specifically for mayors to use in support of such activities. An aide to the Senators is reported as commenting that "the administration is perpetrating a fraud when it says CAAs (community action agencies) can survive revenue sharing."[18] Testifying in 1972 before the Senate Subcommittee on Intergovernmental Relations, which was exploring the concept of "New Federalism" in its broadest contexts (including general and special revenue sharing), Mayor Norman Mineta of San Jose was particularly critical of the effects of revenue sharing on categorical grant programs during the period of transition between the possible elimination of categorical grant programs and the initiation of special revenue-sharing funds. In that testimony, Mayor Minetz stated:

Does the President and his administration seek to help us with the task of transition which lies before us? Have they been trying to help stabilize as many of the community development variables as possible? Absolutely not. In a most insensitive and perhaps even inhuman fashion they have compounded our task of transition by callously freezing, curtailing, abolishing, and repudiating many of the essential elements of our community development effort.[19]

Additional examples of such concerns are vividly reflected in House and Senate hearings held prior to the adoption of the general revenue-sharing bill. Testifying in 1971 before the House Ways and Means Committee considering the bill, a representative of an East Akron OEO-funded neighborhood program bluntly stated: "I know that this plan [General Revenue Sharing] was designed primarily to destroy federal [poverty] programs. . . . Five years ago this nation was in chaos where poor people were concerned. Then there came a program called the Office of Economic Opportunity, where they at least gave them a little of a chance. . . . Revenue sharing would destroy all of this."[20]

The survey conducted for this study asked city officials to indicate whether they would use general revenue-sharing funds to support local programs funded by Model Cities and OEO legislation if these programs were eliminated. Table 5-7 summarizes the responses. It is apparent from Table 5-7 that only a minority of cities definitiely will allocate a portion of general revenue-sharing funds to Model Cities and OEO-funded activities. Although the proportion increased somewhat in the 1974 survey, still less than a third of all cities responded affirmatively. Table 5-8 examines these responses by the various political and environmental factors.

Table 5-7

Use of Revenue-Sharing Funds for OEO and Model Cities Activities

	Will General Revenue Sharing Funds be Used for OEO or Model Cities Activities?[a]					
	Yes		No		Uncertain	
All Cities, 1973	20.8%	(31)	39.6%	(59)	36.6%	(59)
All Cities, 1974	28.2	(40)	33.1	(47)	38.7	(55)

[a]Question answered only by those cities receiving funds from these sources.

Table 5-8 reveals no major deviations in the overall patterns reported in Table 5-7. It is noted that officials in less wealthy, larger central cities are more certain of allocating revenue-sharing funds to OEO and Model Cities programs than are other officials. Perhaps the most interesting information presented in Table 5-8 is that officials of council-manager cities and most reformed cities are more likely to allocate revenue-sharing money to these programs than are officials of mayor-council and least reformed cities. Again, this is in contrast to what would be expected. On the surface, at least, council-manager cities appear to be more responsive to the needs of OEO and Model Cities groups concerning the allocation of revenue-sharing funds. At the same time, it is revealed in Table 5-8 that a much higher proportion of mayor and least reformed cities report a degree of uncertainty concerning the allocation of revenue-sharing funds to these programs. In spite of our findings in Chapter 4, some research would suggest that council-manager cities should be able to reach earlier decisions concerning the allocation of revenue-sharing funds,[21] and it is possible that larger proportions of mayor-council cities will allocate revenue sharing money to these areas once decisions are finalized.

One of the most important conclusions to be drawn from Tables 5-7 and 5-8, then, is that a large number of cities (approximately 40 percent) remain uncertain as to whether general revenue-sharing funds will be allocated to OEO and Model Cities programs. Undoubtedly, this reflects their inability at that time to predict the outcome of the Nixon Administration's special revenue-sharing proposals, and especially those dealing with "better communities." The point to be stressed from Tables 5-7 and 5-8 is that significant proportions of cities do not anticipate the funding of OEO and Model Cities programs from general revenue-sharing funds, and it does appear that without provisions to the contrary, these programs could suffer considerably in any "transition period" from these categorical programs to special revenue-sharing legislation.

Another controversial aspect of general revenue sharing concerns its impact on the taxing efforts of local governments. On the one hand, it is

Table 5-8

Use of Revenue-Sharing Funds for OEO and Model Cities Activities by Political and Environmental Characteristics

Will General Revenue-Sharing Funds be Used for OEO and Model Cities Activities?[a]

	Yes		No		Uncertain	
Total, All Cities	28.2%	(40)	33.1%	(47)	38.7%	(55)
Form of Government						
Mayor	17.4	(8)	23.9	(11)	58.7	(27)
Manager	29.9	(23)	40.2	(31)	29.9	(23)
Municipal Reform[b]						
1	10.0	(2)	10.0	(2)	80.0	(16)
2	20.0	(5)	32.0	(8)	48.0	(12)
3	34.8	(8)	34.8	(8)	30.4	(7)
4	33.9	(21)	38.7	(24)	27.4	(17)
City Size						
50,000 to 100,000	23.8	(15)	39.7	(25)	36.5	(23)
100,000 to 250,000	28.3	(13)	34.7	(16)	37.0	(17)
250,000 to 500,000	38.1	(8)	23.8	(5)	38.1	(8)
Over 500,000	33.3	(4)	8.3	(1)	58.4	(7)
City Type						
Central	30.3	(33)	29.4	(32)	40.3	(44)
Suburban	11.1	(3)	51.9	(14)	37.0	(10)
Region						
Northeast	20.7	(6)	31.0	(9)	48.3	(14)
North Central	30.8	(12)	35.9	(14)	33.3	(13)
South	28.9	(11)	26.3	(10)	44.8	(17)
West	23.3	(7)	43.4	(13)	33.3	(10)
Mean Income						
Less than $10,500	34.5	(20)	29.3	(17)	36.2	(21)
$10,500 to $12,500	25.4	(16)	34.9	(22)	39.7	(25)
Over $12,500	19.0	(4)	38.1	(8)	42.9	(9)
Proportion Non-White						
Less than 5.0%	27.5	(14)	43.1	(22)	29.4	(15)
5.0 to 15.0%	36.6	(15)	26.8	(11)	36.6	(15)
Over 15.0%	22.0	(11)	28.0	(14)	50.0	(25)
Population Change						
Less than 0.0%	26.1	(12)	23.9	(11)	50.0	(23)
0.0 to 25.0%	32.2	(21)	32.3	(21)	35.4	(23)
Over 25.0%	22.6	(7)	48.4	(15)	29.0	(9)

[a]Question answered only by those cities receiving funds from these sources.
[b]The measure of municipal "reformism" used in this study is explained in Appendix C.
Note: Data for this table based on 1974 returns.

clear that some have viewed revenue sharing as a means of lowering, or at least stabilizing, local property taxes. In outlining his early revenue-sharing thesis, Walter Heller argued that the plan "would miss its mark if it did not serve to relieve some of the intense fiscal pressures on local governments" and that it should result "partly into a slowdown of state-local tax increases."[22] Also, it is apparent that a major reason for the strong support President Nixon received for his general revenue-sharing legislation from mayors was their belief that the measure would help prevent increases in property tax rates. Patrick Healy, executive vice president of the National League of Cities, is quoted as saying, "It's okay with us to use the money to reduce taxes because we believe that one of the major problems in cities is that property taxes are too high."[23] President Nixon, himself, on several occasions suggested that general revenue sharing would result in the lowering of state and local taxes. When signing the bill, President Nixon stated that in many states and localities general revenue sharing "will mean lower property taxes or lower sales taxes or lower income taxes than would otherwise have been the case. Revenue sharing can provide desperately needed tax relief for millions of Americans."[24] Earlier, Nixon had remarked that studies by "experts" in the government had estimated that general revenue sharing would result in an across the country reduction in property taxes of approximately 30 percent.[25]

On the other hand, there are those who are critical of an overemphasis of the use of general revenue-sharing funds for tax relief. The argument made by these observers is that the effectiveness of general revenue sharing in fulfilling critical needs of American cities is reduced to the extent that revenue-sharing dollars are applied mainly to a lowering of tax rates. An editorial appearing in the *New York Times,* for example, maintained that cities would use their funds to cut existing taxes without providing new services.[26]

As reported in Chapter 4, in terms of *direct* allocation of general revenue-sharing funds, fears such as those expressed above are largely unwarranted. Only a very small proportion of general revenue sharing funds were applied to direct tax relief. However, it is possible that the funds did help prevent the necessity for increases in tax rates. In this manner, revenue sharing may have had a very significant impact on local tax structures. The surveys conducted for this study asked officials to indicate the effect of revenue sharing on local taxes in 1974 and to indicate the expected long-range tax effect, assuming revenue sharing continues at approximately its current rate. Table 5-9 explores these responses.

Table 5-9 indicates that about 65 percent of the responding officials believed general revenue sharing prevented a tax rate increase or reduced the tax for their cities in fiscal 1974. Interestingly, when considering the long-range effect of general revenue sharing, even a higher proportion of officials believe that it will have a "positive" effect on their tax rates and the largest proportion of these (47.6 percent) believe general revenue sharing will result in a reduction in the amount of tax rate increases.

When considering the effect of revenue sharing on tax rates by the various political and environmental factors (see Table 5-10), a few interest-

Table 5-9
Impact of General Revenue Sharing on Municipal Taxing Levels

Effect of Fiscal Year 1974 Tax Rates

Reduced Tax Rate	Prevented Increase in Tax Rate	Reduced Amount of Rate Increase	No Effect
11.9% (25)	35.8% (75)	17.1% (36)	35.2% (74)

Long-Range Effect on Taxing Levels

Reduce Tax Rate	Prevent Increase in Tax Rate	Reduce Amount of Rate Increase	No Effect
2.4% (5)	27.2% (56)	47.6% (98)	22.8% (47)

ing deviations from these overall patterns are evident. As shown in that Table 5-10, taxing levels were most positively affected in less wealthy, larger central cities. Also, it is interesting to note that the taxing rates in cities in the Northeast were most positively affected. For all categories of cities, the general conclusion would be that revenue sharing has *not* resulted in a reduction of tax rates, but it has contributed to the prevention of *increases* in taxing rates and to reducing the amount of rate increases. Most officials believe that these trends will continue in the future.

Attitudes of Municipal Officials Toward General Revenue Sharing

Finally, it is of interest to examine the attitudes of municipal officials towards general revenue sharing. Chapter 6 examines these issues in depth; here, we are interested only in a general overview of official attitudes toward general revenue sharing. Although mayors strongly supported the Nixon Administration's initial general revenue-sharing proposal, it has been widely reported that many municipal officials are disillusioned with the actual realities of the program. Specifically, it is often reported that mayors fear that if funds for such programs as Community Action Agencies and Model Cities are curtailed, general revenue sharing will result in a net *decrease* in the flow of funds from the federal government to the localities. Mayor Wesley Uhlman of Seattle, for example, testifying before Senator Edmund Muskie's Government Operations Subcommittee on Intergovernmental Relations in February 1973, stated that "general revenue sharing has not turned out to be the savior we had hoped for. . . . I must say that the cities have been deceived. The new federalism has turned out to be a Trojan horse for America's cities. A gift left behind by an administration retreating from its basic responsibilities to the citizens."[27]

Testifying before that same committee, Mayor Henry Maier of Milwaukee stated that "The mayors who campaigned across the country for revenue sharing are really now the victims of a cruel hoax . . . we find the cities to be worse off financially than before revenue sharing was enacted."[28] Expressing a similar view, Mayor Kevin White of Boston in an interview stated: "I am one who fought for the basic tenets of the New Federalism, in the form of general revenue sharing, for the past three years. [Now] I find myself chagrined that I don't know what I have, except that I have less money in the short run and the prospect of less money in the long run."[29]

Although exceptions to these views certainly have been expressed,[30] it is clear that at least some mayors have expressed disappointment with general revenue sharing. Since the Nixon Administration relied so heavily upon the support of mayors in the passage of general revenue sharing, these reservations, if pervasive, may be crucial in the coming legislative debates concerning the renewal of the revenue-sharing legislation. In order to measure the nature and extent of municipal officials' attitudes toward revenue sharing, the surveys asked these officials to estimate the effect general revenue sharing would have on the total amount of federal funds they would receive. Table 5-11 summarizes their responses.

Interestingly, about a third of the officials who responded in 1973 and about 40 percent of those responding in 1974 believed that general revenue sharing will result in a net *decrease* in the total amount of federal funds received by their cities. Thus, the attitudes expressed by some officials, as quoted above, are relatively widespread. Table 5-12 explores these attitudes by the various political and demographic characteristics.

Table 5-12 reveals some rather dramatic differences in the reported effects of revenue sharing on the total amount of federal funds received by the various municipalities. In general, officials of the less wealthy, larger central cities, with larger proportions of non-whites are much more likely to view general revenue sharing as resulting in a net *decrease* in the amount of federal funds to be received by their cities. Perhaps the most pronounced difference is observed when comparing responses by city size. Only 27 percent of the officials of cities between 50,000 and 100,000 believed that revenue sharing will result in a net decrease in federal funds, whereas almost 70 percent of the officials in cities over 250,000 so responded. If these fears are, in fact, warranted, it is obvious that general revenue sharing could have a dramatic effect on federally funded services provided by larger cities.

Table 5-10
Impact of General Revenue Sharing on Municipal Taxing Levels by Political, Demographic, and Environmental Characteristics

	Reduced Tax Rate		Prevented Increase in Tax Rate		Reduced Amount of Rate Increase		No Effect	
Total, All Cities	11.9%	(25)	35.8%	(75)	17.1%	(36)	35.2%	(74)
Form of Government								
Mayor	14.3	(9)	30.2	(19)	31.7	(20)	23.8	(15)
Manager	10.7	(13)	37.2	(45)	11.6	(14)	40.5	(49)
Municipal Reform[a]								
1	18.5	(5)	22.2	(6)	40.8	(11)	18.5	(5)
2	5.4	(2)	27.1	(10)	35.1	(13)	32.4	(12)
3	3.1	(1)	34.4	(11)	6.3	(2)	56.2	(18)
4	16.1	(15)	40.9	(38)	8.6	(8)	34.4	(32)
City Size								
50,000 to 100,000	14.3	(17)	35.3	(42)	15.1	(18)	35.3	(42)
100,000 to 250,000	7.0	(4)	36.8	(21)	17.5	(10)	38.7	(22)
250,000 to 500,000	14.3	(3)	28.6	(6)	23.8	(5)	33.3	(7)
Over 500,000	7.7	(1)	46.1	(6)	23.1	(3)	23.1	(3)

City Type				
Central	12.9 (17)	37.9 (50)	18.2 (24)	31.0 (41)
Suburban	10.0 (7)	31.4 (22)	17.1 (12)	41.5 (29)
Region				
Northeast	21.7 (10)	32.6 (15)	37.0 (17)	8.7 (4)
North Central	8.6 (5)	34.5 (20)	20.7 (12)	36.2 (21)
South	8.0 (4)	50.0 (25)	4.0 (2)	38.0 (19)
West	10.4 (5)	25.0 (12)	10.4 (5)	54.2 (26)
Mean Income				
Less than $10,500	15.2 (12)	40.5 (32)	15.2 (12)	29.1 (23)
$10,500 to $12,500	13.4 (11)	26.8 (22)	20.7 (17)	39.1 (32)
Over $12,500	4.1 (2)	42.8 (21)	14.3 (7)	38.8 (19)
Proportion Non-White				
Less than 5.0%	13.5 (13)	31.3 (30)	19.8 (19)	35.4 (34)
5.0 to 15.0%	15.1 (8)	30.2 (16)	15.1 (8)	39.6 (21)
Over 15.0%	6.6 (4)	47.5 (29)	14.8 (9)	31.1 (19)
Population Change				
Less than 0.0%	14.3 (8)	41.1 (23)	25.0 (14)	19.6 (11)
0.0 to 25.0%	8.8 (9)	38.2 (39)	15.7 (16)	37.3 (38)
Over 25.0%	15.4 (8)	25.0 (13)	11.5 (6)	48.1 (25)

[a]The measure of municipal "reformism" used in this study is explained in Appendix C.

Note: Data in this table are based on 1974 survey.

Table 5-11
Effect of General Revenue-Sharing Funds on Total Federal Funds for Urban Areas

	Greatly Increase		Increase Somewhat		No Effect		Decrease Somewhat		Greatly Decrease	
All Cities, 1973	13.2%	(24)	30.2%	(55)	23.1%	(42)	18.7%	(34)	14.8%	(27)
All Cities, 1974	10.9	(21)	23.3	(45)	26.4	(51)	27.5	(53)	11.9%	(23)

Related to this question, is the overall evaluation of general revenue sharing by city officials. Table 5-13 summarizes the responses to this question. Contrary to what might have been expected given the information presented in Tables 5-11 and 5-12, it is found that those municipal officials responding to this survey are overwhelming in support of general revenue sharing. Over 75 percent of those responding after the receipt of the first three entitlement period funds were "satisfied" or "very satisfied" with general revenue sharing, and over 90 percent responding after the allocation of the fourth entitlement period funds so responded. These proportions seem unusually high, especially when considering the large proportion of officials indicating that revenue sharing would result in a net decrease in the receipt of federal funds. One possible explanation for this apparent discrepancy may be related to the administrative ease with which cities receive and disburse these funds. City agencies are not required to allocate extensive staff time or personnel to meeting regulations or completing applications in the expenditure of general revenue-sharing funds. After the often tedious and demanding requirements of the various grant-in-aid programs, city officials may be particularly pleased with this aspect of the revenue-sharing legislation.

Conclusion

The attitudinal data presented in this chapter provide an analysis of the impact of general revenue sharing beyond that possible through an examination of expenditure data alone. In addition to these policy concerns, these data have significant theoretical implications. This section summarizes several of these.

These data indicate that the expectations by some that general revenue sharing would result in a plethora of bold, new, and creative programs at the local level were overly optimistic. Rather, it was found that over 70 percent of the funds expended to date have been applied to existing, on-going programs and services. Some theoretically interesting deviations in this overall pattern were noted. Manager cities and reformed cities in

Table 5-12

Effect of General Revenue-Sharing Funds on Total Federal Funds for Urban Areas, by Political and Environmental Characteristics

	Increase		No Effect		Decrease	
Total, All Cities	34.2%	(66)	26.4%	(51)	39.4%	(76)
Form of Government						
Mayor	22.4	(13)	25.9	(15)	51.7	(30)
Manager	41.5	(46)	27.9	(31)	30.6	(34)
Municipal Reform[a]						
1	11.5	(3)	30.8	(8)	57.7	(15)
2	28.6	(10)	25.7	(9)	45.7	(16)
3	23.3	(7)	36.7	(11)	40.0	(12)
4	46.0	(40)	24.1	(21)	29.9	(26)
City Size						
50,000 to 100,000	44.9	(48)	28.0	(30)	27.1	(29)
100,000 to 250,000	22.2	(12)	31.5	(17)	46.3	(25)
250,000 to 500,000	15.0	(3)	15.0	(3)	70.0	(14)
Over 500,000	25.0	(3)	8.3	(1)	66.7	(8)
City Type						
Central	23.6	(29)	25.2	(31)	51.2	(63)
Suburban	55.5	(35)	28.6	(18)	15.9	(10)
Region						
Northeast	22.0	(9)	17.0	(7)	61.0	(25)
North Central	42.3	(22)	25.0	(13)	32.7	(17)
South	28.6	(14)	32.7	(16)	38.7	(19)
West	44.4	(20)	28.9	(13)	26.7	(12)
Mean Income						
Less than $10,500	23.6	(17)	20.8	(15)	55.6	(40)
$10,500 to $12,500	36.4	(28)	32.5	(25)	31.1	(24)
Over $12,500	47.7	(21)	25.0	(11)	27.3	(12)
Proportion Non-White						
Less than 5.0%	46.0	(40)	27.6	(24)	26.4	(23)
5.0 to 15.0%	29.2	(14)	22.9	(11)	47.9	(23)
Over 15.0%	20.7	(12)	27.6	(16)	51.7	(30)
Population Change						
Less than 0.0%	16.7	(9)	16.7	(9)	66.6	(36)
0.0 to 25.0%	37.0	(34)	29.3	(27)	33.7	(31)
Over 25.0%	41.8	(23)	41.8	(23)	16.4	(9)

[a]The measure of municipal "reformism" used in this study is explained in Appendix C.
Note: Data in this table are based on the 1974 survey.

general were more likely to spend their funds in new program areas. On the surface, at least, this would lend some support to the general assumption that more centralized political structures are more capable of creative and innovative policy making. However, it is known that to some extent, form of government is a function of demographic variables, and when examining the environmental factors associated with general revenue-sharing spend-

Table 5-13
Respondent Satisfaction with General Revenue Sharing

	Very Satisfied		Somewhat Satisfied		Uncertain		Somewhat Dissatisfied		Very Dissatisfied	
All Cities, 1973	45.3%	(91)	32.3%	(65)	13.4%	(27)	6.0%	(12)	3.0%	(6)
All Cities, 1974	62.1	(121)	28.2	(55)	3.6	(7)	5.1	(10)	1.0%	(2)

ing, it was found that these also are strongly related to the innovative use of such funds. Thus, the expenditure of general revenue-sharing funds on new or on-going programs appears to be a function of "need" (as indicated by such variables as city size, proportion non-white, mean income, and so forth) rather than of political or administrative structure. Less wealthy, large central cities, with higher proportions of non-white population and low or declining population rates were more likely to use their funds to bolster on-going programs. These, of course, are the very cities most directly affected by the "fiscal crises" so often discussed in the late 1960s and early 1970s. It might be assumed that as the fiscal crisis of American cities subsides, as many have predicted, more cities will spend larger proportions of their revenue-sharing funds on new and creative program areas.

It is particularly interesting to note the extent of citizen participation in the expenditure of revenue-sharing funds. It was found, as noted above, that almost 50 percent of those officials responding in 1973 and close to 60 percent of those responding in 1974 indicated that their cities had encouraged some form of direct citizen involvement in their revenue-sharing allocation decisions. Also, it was found that about half of the cities intend to continue this practice in the future. These statistics are especially interesting when it is recalled that unlike many of the major municipal-oriented federal programs of the 1960s, the revenue-sharing legislation includes no specific requirements for citizen input. Perhaps this may be interpreted as indicating that citizen groups, which have become activated in the past several years, will remain strong and viable forces in urban politics.

This examination of revenue-sharing allocations also provided an opportunity to examine the consequences of citizen input. One of the major gaps in the citizen participation literature concerns the ability of such participation to actually effect alterations in decisions.[31] Reviewing much of the OEO and Model Cities literature, John Strange concludes that although many observers claim to have documented policy changes brought about by citizen participation activities, "the causes of such changes and their extent are impossible to document."[32] Our study did detect important differences in the allocations of revenue-sharing funds between those cities holding and those not holding public hearings. As reported above, cities not holding public hearings were much more likely to spend their revenue-sharing funds on public safety functions; cities holding public hearings were more likely to spend their funds for such functions as street and road repair, parks and recreation, social services, and health programs. Although, as suggested above, these data do not "prove" that citizen participation caused such differences, they do provide prima facie evidence to suggest that such participation is associated with objective changes in policy decisions.[33]

It was found that the potential impact of general revenue sharing may be the greatest concerning its effect on Model Cities and OEO-funded activities. It is clear from the discussion presented above that many have been concerned with the implications of general revenue sharing for these programs and to a large extent these data confirm such fears. Only a small proportion of cities indicated that they would use general revenue-sharing funds to support these activities if Model Cities and OEO legislation are phased out. Of course, this does not mean that these activities will not be supported in the future, even if they are phased out of the federal budget, since special revenue-sharing programs may become available for these programs. However, these data do indicate that any "transition period" between cutoffs in the categorical grant programs and the passage of special revenue-sharing programs would create severe financial problems for such programs and for those who benefit from them.

As predicted by its supporters, it was found that about two-thirds of the responding officials believed that general revenue sharing had resulted in the prevention of a tax increase or the reduction in the amount of tax increases. It was also found that about a third of all officials in 1973 and about 40 percent in 1974 expected general revenue sharing to result in a net loss of federal funds received by their cities; however, these officials were overwhelmingly in support of the general revenue-sharing concept.

Finally, it might be noted that the data presented in this chapter indicate that the impact of general revenue sharing on American cities can be discussed largely in terms of two broad categories of municipalities: those that are the less wealthy, large central cities; and those that are the more wealthy, small suburban areas. It is apparent that the impact of revenue sharing on the first category of cities has been qualitatively different from its impact on the second. Table 5-14 summarizes much of the impact data presented in this chapter in terms of these two broad categories of municipalities.

Officials of less wealthy, large central cities are more likely to allocate their general revenue-sharing funds to on-going programs; to hold public hearings prior to the allocation of general revenue-sharing money; to indicate that general revenue-sharing funds will be used to support OEO and Model Cities programs, if necessary; to indicate that general revenue sharing has resulted in the reduction in tax rate increases; and to believe

Table 5-14
Consequences of Revenue Sharing: A Summary of Overall Trends, by Categories of Cities

Consequences	Categories of Cities	
	Less Wealthy Large Central Cities	More Wealthy Small Suburban Cities
Use of Funds?	Existing Programs	New Programs
Public Hearings?	Yes	No
Support of OEO and Model City Activities?	Yes	No
Impact on Taxing Levels?	Lowered Taxing Levels	No Effect
Effect on Receipt of Federal Funds?	Decrease	Increase

Note: This table represents overall trends and is not necessarily indicative of any single city.

that general revenue sharing will result in a net decrease in the receipt of federal funds. These data relate directly to the question raised by many as to whether general revenue-sharing funds have been spread too thinly among local units of government. This survey was limited to the 409 American cities over 50,000; however, revenue-sharing checks were received by almost every general purpose government in the United States (over 38,000 units of government). Even from this study of the most populous cities, it is clear that the impact of general revenue sharing on the largest of these was different from its impact on the smallest. Most significantly, perhaps, it is observed that the less wealthy, large central cities not only found it necessary to spend their funds for the support of on-going (rather than new) programs but also perceived of the general revenue-sharing concept as resulting in a net decrease of federal funds. A recent survey of members of Congress has examined the question of whether Senators and Representatives believe the general revenue-sharing funds were too thinly spread among the thousands of units of local government. Significantly, 52 percent of those responding did *not* agree that general revenue-sharing money was too thinly spread; however, Democrats were much more likely to agree than Republicans (46 to 14 percent).[34]

Of course, the data collected and analyzed for this study do not "prove" either perspective to be correct. However, it must be noted that larger central cities are having to spend a disproportionate amount of their general revenue-sharing checks simply to maintain on-going programs, and one cannot avoid the conclusion that the largest cities could benefit from a share of general revenue-sharing funds greater than that allotted by the present formula. It seems certain that this is one issue that cannot be avoided in future legislative debates.

Notes

1. Bill Kovach, "Revenue Sharing Assailed as Going to Wrong Places," *New York Times,* February 21, 1973.

2. The entire text of President Nixon's 1971 State of the Union message can be found in the *Congressional Quarterly Almanac, 1971.*

3. The entire text of President Nixon's 1972 State of the Union message can be found in the *Congressional Quarterly Almanac, 1972.*

4. See, for example, the article entitled "Nixon's New Federalism': Struggle to Prove Itself," appearing in the *Washington Post,* June 17, 1973, by Lou Cannon and David S. Broder.

5. Robert L. Crain, Elihu Katz, and Donald B. Rosenthal, *The Politics of Community Conflict: The Fluoridation Decision* (Indianapolis: Bobbs-Merrill, 1969).

6. Michael Aiken and Robert R. Alford, "Community Structure and Innovation: The Case of Public Housing," *American Political Science Review* 64 (September 1970), pp. 843-864.

7. An explanation of the measure of reformism used in this study is found in Appendix C.

8. See, for example, the article by Raymond E. Wolfinger and John O. Field, "Political Ethos and the Structure of City Government," *American Political Science Review* 60 (June 1966), pp. 306-26.

9. The Tax Foundation predicts that by 1975 state and local governments will realize a $12.6 billion surplus.

10. With the stipulation, of course, that such funds are to be spent in "priority areas" as defined by the legislation.

11. A summary of the comments of Reverend Jackson may be found in *Information Bulletin No. 74-4,* published by the Advisory Commission on Intergovernmental Relations, Washington, D.C., May, 1974.

12. This phrase was used in President Nixon's 1972 State of the Union Address and quoted in the *Congressional Quarterly Almanac, 1972,* p. 9-A.

13. A summary of the comments of Mayor Richard Hatcher may be found in *Information Bulletin No. 74-4,* published by the Advisory Commission on Intergovernmental Relations, Washington, D.C., May, 1974.

14. For a comprehensive examination of citizen participation in American cities, see Carl Stenberg, *The New Grass Roots Government?* (Washington, D.C.: Advisory Commission on Intergovernmental Relations, 1972).

15. For a comparison of the various characteristics of manager-council and mayor-council cities, see Edward C. Banfield and James Q. Wilson, *City Politics* (New York, Alfred A. Knopf, 1963), chapter 11.

16. Peter Eisinger has recently dealt with the "open" and "closed" characteristics of the various forms of local government. See his article, "The Conditions of Protest Behavior in American Cities," *American Political Science Review* 67 (March 1973), pp. 11-29.

17. As quoted in the *Congressional Quarterly Weekly Report*, March 10, 1971, p. 63-A.

18. As reported in the *Congressional Quarterly Weekly Report*, March 10, 1973, p. 506.

19. U.S. Congress, Senate, Subcommittee on Intergovernmental Relations of the Committee on Government Operations, *A New Federalism*, 93rd. Congress, 1st Sess., February 21, 23, 27, 28 and March 8, 14, 15, 1973, p. 29.

20. U.S. Congress, House, Committee on Ways and Means, *General Revenue Sharing*, 92nd Congress, 1st Sess., June 21, 23, and 24, 1971, p. 1308.

21. See Crain, Katz, and Rosenthal, *The Politics of Community Conflict*.

22. Walter W. Heller, *New Dimensions of Political Economy* (Cambridge, Mass.: Harvard University Press, 1966), p. 152.

23. As quoted in *National Journal*, April 3, 1971, p. 732.

24. From President Nixon's statement when signing the general revenue-sharing bill in Philadelphia, October 20, 1972.

25. From President Nixon's remarks to Eastern media executives attending a briefing on domestic policy in Rochester, New York, June 18, 1971.

26. Editorial appearing in the *New York Times*, October 17, 1972, p. 4, col. 1.

27. U.S. Congress, Senate, Subcommittee on Intergovernmental Relations of the Committee on Government Operations, *A new Federalism*, 93rd Congress, 1st Sess., February 21, 23, 27, 28 and March 8, 14, 15, 1973, p. 67.

28. Ibid. p. 21.

29. As quoted by Lou Cannon and David S. Broder, "Nixon's 'New Federalism': Struggle to Prove Itself," *The Washington Post*, June 17, 1973.

30. See the full text of the article in the *Congressional Quarterly Weekly Report*, March 3, 1973, pp. 471-3.

31. For a review of much of this literature as well as an attempt to demonstrate impact of citizen participation, see Richard L. Cole, *Citizen Participation and the Urban Policy Process* (Lexington, Mass.: D.C. Heath, Lexington Books, 1974), pp. 103-6.

32. John Strange, "The Impact of Citizen Participation on Public Administration," *Public Administration Review,* 32 (September,72), pp. 457-470.

33. It would be interesting to examine the citizen participation programs themselves to determine whether different types of citizen input have differing impacts. The data collected for this study do not allow such comparisons.

34. U.S. Congress, House, Intergovernmental Relations Subcommittee of the Committee on Government Operations, *Replies by Members of Congress to a Questionnaire on General Revenue Sharing,* 93rd Congress, 2nd Sess., April, 1974.

6

Partisan Politics and Coalition Building: The Future of General Revenue Sharing

Introduction

The tempo of the public debate, which general revenue sharing has already attracted, is likely to continue at an increasing rate in the near future. Certainly one of the more complex public decisions that will be made by the Congress and President Gerald Ford in the coming months concerns the future of general revenue sharing. The alternatives are basically clear, and regardless of which are chosen, the results will have significant political impact on the American public. These are the key decisions that must be made:

1. For how long and at what funding level should general revenue sharing be continued?[1]
2. Should the distribution formulas be changed so as to emphasize population and structural disparities among the various units of government?[2]
3. Should general revenue-sharing funds continue to be received by nearly all general purpose units of government, or should the distribution be restricted or, perhaps even expanded to include special district governments?[3]
4. Should the present restrictions on the use of general revenue-sharing funds in the several "priority areas" be expanded or restricted?[4]
5. Should the Office of Revenue Sharing and other federal agencies take more active roles in assuring compliance, and should the recipients have greater administrative requirements in order to receive the funds?[5]
6. Should there be legislative and/or administrative requirements specifying the form and nature of citizen participation in the general revenue-sharing decision-making process?[6]

While the answers to these questions may appear uncomplicated, they will require exceedingly difficult political negotiation and compromise among the many participants. This chapter considers several of the more important political questions and coalitions that might develop during the upcoming legislative process and the possible outcome of that process.

As was the case concerning the passage of the initial general revenue-sharing legislation, the upcoming process will be affected by a wide range of political and environmental factors. Three of the more important of these factors will be (1) the fiscal situation of American cities; (2) the general nature of city life during the legislative process; and (3) the tides of national politics.

To begin with, if the leaders of the cities are able to convince the public and the national decision makers that they are in fact confronted with impending or actual fiscal disaster, the chances of a sympathetic hearing will increase. The widely held feeling that cities were indeed in a fiscal straitjacket was important in passing the initial legislation. A key point to be stressed in the consideration of a general revenue-sharing extension will be inflation. As Mayor Moon Landrieu of New Orleans, in his role as Vice-Chairman of the Community Development Committee for the National League of Cities, stated to the Senate Government Operations Subcommittee on Intergovernmental Relations in June 1974: "the 'urban crisis' has not disappeared. It is with us and current trends indicate that the fiscal crisis of the cities is deepening. . . . Inflation is having a devastating impact on municipal budgets. . . . We thus find ourselves being squeezed to a maximum. Expenditures are once again rapidly outstripping our ability to generate revenues."[7] Landrieu's remarks illustrate the feeling expressed by six large city mayors at the National Conference of Mayor's meeting in San Diego in June 1974.[8]

With the need to increase municipal salaries and to keep services at the same level despite inflation, many cities have been faced with difficult financial decisions. Obviously this will be a factor when spokesman for the cities attempt to justify their needs. Related to this will be the result of the various special revenue-sharing measures called for by the Nixon Administration.[9] Mayor Landrieu stressed this relationship when he stated: "We are striving for an adequately funded and properly balanced assistance program to municipal governments. General revenue sharing, block grants, and categoricals are each essential components of that system. They must not be viewed in conflict."[10] As pointed out in Chapter 3, the special revenue-sharing measures are designed to return federal funds to the cities in the form of block grants with the individual city then having general discretionary power to use those funds as needed or desired. Manpower special revenue-sharing funds have been received by most jurisdictions, while housing and community development legislation was passed and signed into law in August, 1974. Obviously, the effects of these programs will influence the general fiscal setting of the cities.

A second and critical environmental factor will involve the general condition of city life. By this is meant the presence and frequency of urban protest and violence. If these are relatively absent, then the decision makers could be less inclined to respond to the differential needs exacerbated by diverse economic and social cleavages. If there is a recurrence of the violence and unrest that marked the 1960s, one result may be a decision-making process marked with emotion and less concern for more objective thought in reaching major decisions.

There is yet another aspect of the nature of city life that may have significant influence during the general revenue-sharing legislative debate. This involves the role citizen groups are to play in future revenue-sharing decisions. Mayor Landrieu both anticipated and summarized the upcoming debate on this point, when he stated:

Over the past 11 years, local officials have had a great deal of experience with direct citizen participation. Revenue sharing is once again focusing attention on this important issue—local officials welcome this increased concern and involvement in community affairs. . . . Revenue sharing can serve as a useful citizen participation catalyst, but local budgetary decisions must be made within the context of the total revenues available. . . . We have heard that certain groups here in Washington would like to see a special citizen participation mechanism attached to the revenue-sharing program. This we would have to oppose. In the final analysis, revenue-sharing dollars must be evaluated along with the other available local revenues. Decisions on priorities cannot be treated outside of the overall budgetary process.[11]

Thus, the stage is set for debate and ultimate decision on the role of citizen participation in general revenue-sharing decision making. Local citizen groups and social agencies will have to muster a significant lobbying effort in order to deal effectively with this point. Whether in fact this is done and its ultimate effectiveness will be an extremely interesting aspect of the upcoming legislative debate.[12]

Finally, any consideration of general revenue sharing will be greatly affected by the political tides at work in the United States.[13] Certainly the national mood will have an impact. With President Nixon's resignation, a chief spokesman for general revenue sharing has been removed, and President Ford's position and enthusiasm for the program is uncertain at present. Should he decide to attempt to reduce inflation by reducing government spending, general revenue sharing may be a casualty, since the initial legislation passed only after considerable administration pressure and at a time when President Nixon's popularity was at an all time high. Undoubtedly, the political decisions and preparations underway for the 1976 elections will have some influence on the legislative process and especially for general revenue sharing. If key legislative leaders, such as Senators Muskie, Kennedy, Jackson or Congressmen Mills, Reuss, or Fountain decide their political fortunes are associated with the general revenue-sharing legislation, then the decision-making process could well be set in a different perspective. The importance of individual needs and party issues will have a bearing on the decisions ultimately reached. One additional factor, the impact of Watergate and its effect in determining electoral outcomes, cannot be ignored.

The November 1974 congressional elections are being cited as the first national test of the public's response to the events of Watergate and Richard M. Nixon's historic resignation from the presidency. If the elections, especially those involving the House of Representatives, were to result in a large net gain for either party (the accepted assumption is that this can only happen to the Democrats), the subsequent legislative debate and action could be vastly different depending upon which specific seats are won and lost. If a sufficient number of newly elected officials emerge from the November elections, the outcome of the revenue-sharing legislation may be considerably affected.

While these and other aspects of national developments doubtlessly will have an impact on general revenue sharing, the feelings, wants, and needs of the program recipients at the local government level will also have a decided impact. Before considering possible coalitions and strategies, it would be useful to consider the level of funding and satisfaction perceived by decision makers in cities over 50,000.

Recipient Satisfaction

One item in each survey asked the various respondents to indicate their overall satisfaction with general revenue sharing. Table 6-1 summarizes the responses for 1973 and 1974. As indicated by the table entries, city leaders initially were satisfied with general revenue sharing and were even more satisfied with the program in 1974. Note that the percentage "very satisfied" increased from 45.3 percent in 1973 to 62.1 percent in 1974, while the percentage "very dissatisfied" dropped from 3.0 percent in 1973 to 1.0 percent in 1974. Even for a program actively sought by most city officials (see Chapter 3), the level of support indicated in Table 6-1 is remarkable. There is little doubt that general revenue sharing is quite popular among city officials and that this popularity is increasing. As Mayor Landrieu, in his role as spokesman for the nation's mayors stated: "The single overriding message we are determined to leave with this committee, and to leave with the entire Congress, is that the nation's cities continue to be 100 percent united in their support of the general revenue-sharing program."[14]

In terms of size, Table 6-1 offers several interesting perspectives. Note that cities in the 50,000 to 100,000 and 100,000 to 250,000 ranges were most likely to be "very satisfied" with programs in both 1973 and 1974, while the largest percentage of "uncertain" responses in 1973 were from cities in the 250,000 to 500,000 and over 500,000 categories. Also note that leaders in cities in the 250,000 to 500,000 category were less likely in 1974 to feel "very satisfied" with the program. This is an interesting aspect related to size and probably reflects the uncertainty of the decision-making process regarding categorical grant continuation and special revenue-sharing legislation.

The size differential affecting attitudes is not reflected in the data for central and suburban types of cities. In 1973, 44.4 percent of the leaders in central cities and 47.3 percent of the suburban leaders were "very satisfied" with the program. These percentages increased to 65.0 and 59.7 respectively in 1974 and support the contention that city type does not have a significant effect on attitudes toward general revenue sharing.

Region appears to have the largest effect on respondent satisfaction. Southern leaders were initially, and remain, the most satisfied with the program, while respondents in the North Central and Northeastern states were less likely to be "very satisfied" with the program. Interestingly, the greatest shift in regional attitudes occurred in Western cities that increased their percent responding "very satisfied" from 38.5 percent in 1973 to 66.0 percent in 1974. The generally lower satisfaction level in Northeastern and North Central cities is probably related to a variety of factors, but most important among these may be the quantity of demands upon the governments and their concern over a reduction in federal categorical grant programs. Whatever the reasons in 1973, they were substantially eliminated in 1974.

Based on the findings in Table 6-1, it may be possible to speculate on the future attitudes and coalitions that may develop in support of general revenue sharing. First, it is obvious there will not be widespread, or even more than token, opposition to the general revenue-sharing concept and program among local officials. Second, size and metropolitan type variations will not result in different support levels for the program. Finally, regional differences, although declining, may be associated with cities in the Northeastern and North Central regions attempting to alter various provisions of the legislation in order to increase their level of satisfaction with the program. Table 6-2 summarizes respondent satisfaction by form of government. Interestingly, respondents in council-manager cities were more likely to be "very satisfied" with the program in both 1973 and 1974 than were respondents in mayor-council cities. The number of "very dissatisfied" respondents was the same (3 in 1973 and 1 in 1974) in both mayor-council and council-manager cities. Finally, note the decrease in the number of "uncertain" responses and the fact that respondents in council-manager cities were more likely to be uncertain than respondents in mayor-council cities.

Another perspective of the impact of governmental structure is gained by examining the responses by city reform scores. Table 6-3 does this. Perhaps the most interesting aspect of Table 6-3 is the lack of increase in the number of "very satisfied" respondents from 1973 to 1974 (12 in both years) for the least reformed cities, while all of the other cities, regardless of

Table 6-1
Respondent Satisfaction with General Revenue Sharing and City Size, Region, and Type

Response 1973 N = 201 1974 N = 195	Very Satisfied				Somewhat Satisfied				Uncertain			
	1973 %	No.	1974 %	No.	1973 %	No.	1974 %	No.	1973 %	No.	1974 %	No.
Total, All Cities	45.3	91	62.1	121	32.3	65	28.2	55	13.4	27	3.6	7
Population Group												
Over 500,000	41.7	5	60.0	6	25.0	3	30.0	3	25.0	3	—	—
250,000 to 500,000	37.5	6	42.2	8	25.0	4	36.8	7	31.3	5	10.5	2
100,000 to 250,000	40.4	21	66.6	36	40.4	21	29.6	16	9.6	5	1.9	1
50,000 to 100,000	48.7	59	63.4	71	30.6	37	25.9	29	11.6	14	3.6	4
Region												
Northeast	42.5	17	59.0	23	30.0	12	28.1	11	15.0	6	2.6	1
North Central	30.5	14	56.6	30	43.5	20	32.0	17	15.2	7	3.8	2
South	60.3	35	70.8	34	25.9	15	27.1	13	13.8	8	—	—
West	38.5	20	66.0	31	34.6	18	19.1	9	11.5	6	8.5	4
Metropolitan Type												
Central City	44.3	56	65.0	78	31.0	39	24.2	29	15.9	20	4.2	5
Suburban	47.3	35	59.7	40	35.1	26	31.3	21	8.1	6	3.0	2

Response 1973 N = 201 1974 N = 195	Somewhat Dissatisfied				Very Dissatisfied			
	1973 %	No.	1974 %	No.	1973 %	No.	1974 %	No.
Total, All Cities	6.0	12	5.1	10	3.0	6	1.0	2
Population Group								
Over 500,000	—	—	10.0	1	8.3	1	—	—
250,000 to 500,000	—	—	10.5	2	6.2	1	—	—
100,000 to 250,000	9.6	5	1.9	1	—	—	1.8	2
50,000	5.8	7	5.3	6	3.3	4	—	—
Region								
Northeast	12.5	5	10.3	4	—	—	—	—
North Central	6.5	3	5.7	3	4.3	2	1.9	1
South	—	—	2.1	1	—	—	—	—
West	7.7	4	4.3	2	7.7	4	2.1	1
Metropolitan Type								
Central City	5.6	7	5.8	7	3.2	4	.8	1
Suburban	6.8	5	4.5	3	2.7	2	1.5	1

Note: Percentages computed from number of respondents answering question. Row totals equal 100.0 percent.

Table 6-2
Respondent Satisfaction with General Revenue Sharing and Form of Government

Form of Government	Very Satisfied				Somewhat Satisfied				Uncertain			
	1973		1974		1973		1974		1973		1974	
	%	No.	%	No.	%	No.	%	No.	%	No.	%	No.
Mayor-Council	38.9	26	58.2	32	29.8	20	29.1	16	20.9	14	1.8	1
Council-Manager	48.4	59	65.5	74	33.6	41	28.3	32	9.8	12	3.5	4

Form of Government	Somewhat Dissatisfied				Very Dissatisfied			
	1973		1974		1973		1974	
	%	No.	%	No.	%	No.	%	No.
Mayor-Council	6.0	4	9.1	5	4.4	3	1.8	1
Council-Manager	5.7	7	1.8	2	2.5	3	.9	1

Note: Percentages computed from number of respondents answering question. Row totals equal 100.0 percent.

structure, were experiencing marked percentage increases in their level of satisfaction. This would tend to indicate that mayors in the most partisan cities were not experiencing the same increase in satisfaction with general revenue sharing as respondents in the other cities were. If this trend continues, it may result in an extensive effort by these mayors to bring about changes during the next legislative debate on general revenue sharing. When compared with Table 6-2, the finding is even more interesting and probably indicates, as Wolfinger and Field have argued, that non-reform cities may have unique characteristics from cities with differing structural organization. Also, note that cities with a reform score of 2 increased their level of satisfaction (37.2 percent in 1973 to 48.7 percent in 1974) at a slower rate than did cities with reform scores of 3 and 4. This reinforces the contention that while there is support for general revenue sharing in the less reformed cities, the level of support is markedly less than in the more reformed cities.

Demographic characteristics of the cities are often useful in analyzing attitudinal as well as expenditure data. Table 6-4 summarizes respondent satisfaction by cities and percent non-white population, income, and population change. It is found that these variables have less effect on respondent satisfaction than do the variables presented in Tables 6-1 and 6-2. Interestingly, cities with mean incomes under $10,500 reported the greatest initial satisfaction (54.1 percent) with general revenue sharing; in 1974, cities with mean income over $12,500 were most satisfied (66.6 percent) with general revenue sharing. The changes between 1973 and 1974 levels of satisfaction are probably best interpreted as an . initial uncertainty on the part of those cities with mean incomes over $10,500. Once they had received funds from and gained experience in the general revenue-sharing program, their level of satisfaction sharply increased.

Non-white population does have a direct bearing on the level of satisfaction in both 1973 and 1974. Those cities with non-white populations over 15 percent were the least likely to have strong satisfaction (40.3 percent) towards general revenue sharing in 1974, while over 50 percent of the cities with less than 5 percent non-white population reported being "very satisfied" with the program. An interesting shift occurred from 1973 to 1974 in cities with non-white population between 5 and 15 percent. These city officials had a low percentage of "very satisfied" attitudes in 1973 (41.2 percent) and the largest percent in 1974 (72.4 percent). It appears that leaders in cities with significant non-white population may not be as enthusiastic about general revenue sharing due to the many demands upon them and the greater needs of their citizenry for socially oriented programs. Thus, they may be pleased with the program but at the same time feel more could be done through both general revenue sharing and other legislative programs.

Table 6-3
Respondent Satisfaction with General Revenue Sharing and Structural Organization

Response
1973 N = 190
1974 N = 177

Reform Score[a]	Very Satisfied				Somewhat Satisfied				Uncertain			
	1973		1974		1973		1974		1973		1974	
	%	No.	%	No.	%	No.	%	No.	%	No.	%	No.
1	52.2	12	52.2	12	30.5	7	34.8	8	4.3	1	—	—
2	37.2	6	48.7	18	20.9	9	40.5	15	27.9	12	2.7	1
3	41.7	15	63.3	19	30.5	11	30.0	9	19.4	7	—	—
4	47.7	42	71.3	62	39.8	35	18.4	16	6.8	6	6.9	6

Response
1973 N = 190
1974 N = 177

Reform Score[a]	Somewhat Dissatisfied				Very Dissatisfied			
	1973		1974		1973		1974	
	%	No.	%	No.	%	No.	%	No.
1	8.7	2	13.0	3	4.3	1	—	—
2	9.3	4	5.4	2	4.7	2	2.7	1
3	5.6	2	6.7	2	2.8	1	—	—
4	3.4	3	2.3	2	2.3	2	1.1	1

[a]For a discussion of the reform scores, see Appendix C.

Note: Percentages computed from number of respondents answering question. Row totals equal 100.0 percent.

Population change appears to have little relationship to level of satisfaction. Cities that lost population and those that were growing most rapidly had the greatest increase in "very satisfied" attitudes from 1973 to 1974, while there was not a great deal of difference in the percent "very satisfied" in all three categories for both years.

In sum, then, it appears that initial uncertainty and doubt concerning general revenue sharing has been replaced with increasing satisfaction towards the program. Fewer respondents report dissatisfaction and uncertainty about the program in 1973 than in 1974 and over half of the respondents, regardless of their city's demographic characteristics, are very satisfied with the program. Mayors in the most partisan cities are an exception in that the number reporting "very satisfied" has remained constant in the two years the program has been in existence.

Although it is tempting to speculate on the coalitions that will develop in support of general revenue sharing based on the data presented in Tables 6-1 and 6-4, another factor must be taken into account. What do the city officials perceive the effect of general revenue sharing on the total amount of federal funds coming into their cities? Before considering the possible political coalitions, responses to this question will be summarized.

Table 6-5 indicates that respondents did *not* perceive general revenue-sharing funds as greatly increasing the total amount of federal funds they would be receiving. Interestingly, the percentage believing general revenue-sharing funds would increase total federal funds actually fell from 13.2 percent to 10.9 percent in the "greatly increase" and from 30.2 percent to 23.3 percent in the "increase somewhat" categories from 1973 to 1974. There was a decline in the "greatly decrease" category from 1973 to 1974, but increases in the "no effect" and "decrease somewhat" categories. It would appear that city leaders have not drastically altered their views on the effect of general revenue sharing on total federal funds. It is also apparent that city leaders did not envision general revenue sharing as resulting in a large net gain of federal revenues for their cities. If this is the case, perhaps the explanation for the high evaluation of revenue sharing reported above relates to the general unrestricted nature of the use of the funds and the minimal administrative requirements associated with the program. These could have significant impact on the attitudes of city officials who have had long experience in dealing with federal programs that in their view may have had rigid requirements and provided little, if any, local autonomy. In addition to this overall tendency, there are a number of interesting relationships in Table 6-5.

Note the large increase in respondents in all cities regardless of size in the "decrease somewhat" category. Only cities in the 250,000 to 500,000 category did not have a large percentage increase in those responding this way. This is in contrast with the percentage increase in the "greatly

Table 6-4
Repondent Satisfaction with General Revenue Sharing and Demographic Variables

Response 1973 N = 213 1974 N = 216 Variable	Very Satisfied				Somewhat Satisfied				Uncertain			
	1973		1974		1973		1974		1973		1974	
	%	No.	%	No.	%	No.	%	No.	%	No.	%	No.
Income												
Less than $10,500	54.1	39	63.6	49	29.2	21	29.9	23	13.9	10	1.3	1
$10,500 to $12,500	39.4	34	57.9	44	32.6	28	27.7	21	16.3	14	5.3	4
Over $12,500	41.9	18	66.6	28	37.2	16	26.2	11	7.0	3	4.8	2
Non-White Population												
Less than 5%	50.7	44	62.2	56	29.9	26	26.7	24	10.3	9	5.6	5
5% to 15%	41.2	21	72.4	34	37.3	19	17.0	8	15.7	8	2.1	1
Over 15%	40.3	25	52.5	30	32.3	20	40.4	23	16.1	10	1.8	1
Population Change												
Less than 0%	41.2	23	64.0	32	35.7	20	28.0	14	14.2	8	4.0	2
0% to 25%	47.5	40	58.9	56	28.6	24	30.5	29	16.7	14	3.2	3
More than 25%	45.9	28	66.0	33	34.4	21	24.0	12	8.2	5	4.0	2

Response 1973 N = 213 1974 N = 216 Variable	Somewhat Dissatisfied				Very Dissatisfied			
	1973 %	No.	1974 %	No.	1973 %	No.	1974 %	No.
Income								
Less than $10,500	2.8	2	5.2	4	—	—	—	1
$10,500 to $12,500	7.0	6	7.9	6	4.7	4	1.2	1
Over $12,000	9.3	4	2.4	1	4.6	2	—	—
Non-White Population								
Less than 5%	5.7	5	4.4	4	3.4	3	1.1	1
5% to 15%	3.8	2	6.4	3	2.0	1	2.1	1
Over 15%	8.1	5	5.3	3	3.2	2	—	—
Population Change								
Less than 0%	8.9	5	4.0	2	—	—	—	1
0% to25%	3.6	3	6.3	6	3.6	3	1.1	1
More than 25%	6.6	4	4.0	2	4.9	3	2.0	1

Note: Percentages computed from number of respondents answering questions. Row totals equal 100.0%.

Table 6-5
Effect of General Revenue-Sharing Funds on Total Federal Funds, by City Size, Region, and Type

Responses 1973 N = 213 1974 N = 216	Greatly Increase				Increase Somewhat				No Effect			
	1973		1974		1973		1974		1973		1974	
	%	No.	%	No.	%	No.	%	No.	%	No.	%	No.
Total, all cities	13.2	24	10.9	21	30.2	55	23.3	45	23.1	42	26.4	51
Population Group												
Over 500,000	9.1	1	7.7	1	54.5	6	23.1	3	9.1	1	7.7	1
250,000 to 500,000	—	—	—	—	13.3	2	15.0	3	13.3	2	15.0	3
100,000 to 250,000	9.6	5	3.7	2	25.0	13	18.5	10	28.9	15	31.5	17
50,000 to 100,000	17.3	18	17.8	19	32.7	34	27.1	29	23.1	24	28.0	30
Region												
Northeast	11.8	4	9.8	4	14.7	5	12.2	5	35.2	12	17.0	7
North Central	13.6	6	11.8	6	31.8	14	29.3	15	25.0	11	25.5	13
South	13.0	7	8.1	4	37.0	20	20.4	10	14.8	8	32.7	16
West	14.0	7	13.3	6	32.0	16	31.1	14	22.0	11	28.9	13
Metropolitan Type												
Central City	6.8	8	4.9	6	30.8	36	18.7	23	20.5	24	25.2	31
Suburban	25.0	16	22.2	14	29.7	19	33.3	21	26.6	17	28.6	18

Note: Percentages computed from number of respondents answering question. Row totals equal 100.0 percent.

Responses 1973 N = 213 1974 N = 216	Decrease Somewhat				Greatly Decrease			
	1973		1974		1973		1974	
	%	No.	%	No.	%	No.	%	No.
Total, All Cities	18.7	34	27.5	53	14.8	27	11.9	23
Population Group								
Over 500,000	18.2	2	46.1	6	9.1	1	15.4	2
250,00 to 500,000	46.7	7	25.0	5	26.7	4	45.0	9
100,000 to 250,000	17.3	9	31.5	17	19.2	10	14.8	8
50,000 to 100,000	15.4	16	23.4	25	11.5	12	3.7	4
Region								
Northeast	11.8	4	39.0	16	26.5	9	22.0	9
North Central	18.2	8	21.6	11	11.4	5	11.8	6
South	18.5	10	32.7	16	16.7	9	6.1	3
West	24.0	12	17.8	8	8.0	4	8.9	4
Metropolitan Type								
Central City	24.8	29	33.3	41	17.1	20	17.9	22
Suburban	7.8	5	15.9	10	10.9	7	—	—

decrease" response for the cities over 250,000 (9.1 percent to 15.4 percent and 21.7 percent to 45.0 percent, respectively) and those under 250,000 (19.2 percent to 14.8 percent and 11.5 percent to 3.7 percent, respectively) between 1973 and 1974. While the results controlling for size are not always consistent, it would appear that there was a slight tendency for smaller cities to view general revenue sharing as having a positive effect on their total federal funds while larger cities were less favorable. This is to be expected as many of the larger cities had extensive federal funding for the various categorical grant programs that were being phased out or were anticipated to be phased out. Thus, many large city officials may have based their feelings on anticipated total federal revenues and were therefore more pessimistic. The smaller cities may have experienced increased federal funds due to general revenue sharing.

Region also provides some interesting speculative points. City leaders in the Northeast were most likely (26.5 percent) to report that general revenue-sharing funds would result in a large net loss of federal funds for their cities in 1973. This negative outlook decreased slightly in 1974 to 22.0 percent believing the net effect would be to "greatly decrease" the amount of federal funds, while the percent indicating a "decrease somewhat" response increased from 11.8 percent to 39.0 percent. Over one-third of the respondents in Southern cities in both 1973 and 1974 indicated that general revenue-sharing funds would decrease the total federal funds they received. North Central respondents were quite consistent in their response rates in 1973 and 1974, while Western respondents varied only slightly in the "no effect" and "decrease somewhat" categories. Earlier discussion indicated that the Northeastern and North Central respondents were least likely to evaluate general revenue sharing most favorably while Southern respondents were most likely to. The data presented in Table 6-5 would indicate that the North Central respondents' more unfavorable evaluation is based on attitudes *not* stemming from their perception of the effect of the funds on total federal funds received.

A review of the metropolitan type categories confirm a widely held view: suburban cities believe that general revenue sharing will have a greater positive effect on total federal funds they receive than do central cities. This was the case in 1973; 6.8 percent of the central cities and 25.0 percent of the suburban cities respondents reported the effect would be to greatly increase total federal funds while these percentages fell to 4.9 percent and 22.2 percent in 1974. The percentage of central cities responding the effect would be to decrease somewhat or greatly the total federal funds they received increased from 41.9 percent in 1973 to 51.2 percent in 1974 for central cities while decreasing from 18.7 percent in 1973 to 15.9 percent in 1974 for suburban cities. This reflects the fact that many of the suburban cities did not participate in the various categorical grant programs to the extent the large cities did and that the large cities are thus fearful that general revenue-sharing funds are meant to be a substitute for categorical grant funds and do not represent a net increase in total federal funds returned to the communities.

Table 6-6 offers an interesting insight into the relationship between form of government and the perception of the effect of general revenue sharing funds on total federal funds. In both 1973 and 1974, respondents from council-manager cities were more likely to believe the effect of general revenue-sharing funds would be more positive than did respondents in mayor-council cities. These same respondents were also more likely to report a general decrease in total federal funds due to general revenue sharing. Despite these minor differences, form of government does not appear to have significant impact on respondent attitudes towards the effect of general revenue-sharing on total federal funds.

Table 6-7 examines the relationship between a city's structural organization and respondents' attitudes on the effect of general revenue-sharing funds on total federal funds. Note that the percent believing that general revenue sharing will cause federal funds to "increase greatly" or "somewhat" decreases for all four types of cities from 1973 to 1974, with the exception of the "increase somewhat" category for cities with reform scores of 2. The decrease is less for cities with reform scores of 3 and 4 and the greatest for cities with reform scores of 1. The end result is that by 1974 only 11.5 percent of the respondents in the least reformed cities reported that general revenue-sharing funds will have a positive effect on total federal funds, while 45.9 percent of the most reformed city respondents hold that view. Apparently respondents in less politicized cities believe general revenue sharing will result in a net gain in federal revenue for them, while the most politicized city leaders feel the effect will be more negative. In fact, 57.7 percent of the 1974 respondents in cities with reform scores of 1 felt that general revenue sharing would result in a net decrease in total federal funds to their cities. This may help to explain why the less reformed cities are indeed less favorable towards general revenue sharing than respondents in the more reformed cities.

One last point should be made concerning Table 6-7; note that the percent believing the net effect of general revenue sharing will be to decrease total federal funds declines as the reform score increases. The pattern in Table 6-7 is much more consistent than the evaluation pattern discussed in Table 6-2 and indicates that degree of reform is clearly associated with perception of net effect of general revenue-sharing funds on total federal funds.

Table 6-8 summarizes the relationship between the socioeconomic

Table 6-6
Effect of General Revenue-Sharing Funds on Total Federal Funds by Form of Government

Form of Government	Greatly Increase		Increase Somewhat		No Effect	
	1973 % No.	1974 % No.	1973 % No.	1974 % No.	1973 % No.	1974 % No.
Mayor-Council	11.8 7	8.6 5	20.3 12	13.8 8	23.8 14	25.9 15
Council-Manager	14.5 16	12.7 14	35.1 39	28.8 32	20.7 23	27.9 31

Form of Government	Decrease Somewhat		Greatly Decrease	
	1973 % No.	1974 % No.	1973 % No.	1974 % No.
Mayor-Council	20.3 12	31.0 18	23.8 14	20.7 12
Council-Manager	18.0 20	24.3 27	11.7 13	6.3 7

Note: Percentages computed from number of respondents answering question. Row totals equal 100.0 percent.

Table 6-7
Effect of General Revenue-Sharing Funds on Total Federal Funds, by Structural Reformism

Responses
1973 N = 213
1974 N = 216

Reform Score[a]	Greatly Increase 1973 (% / No.)	Greatly Increase 1974 (% / No.)	Increase Somewhat 1973 (% / No.)	Increase Somewhat 1974 (% / No.)	1973 (% / No.)	1974 (% / No.)
1	9.3 / 2	7.7 / 2	28.6 / 6	3.8 / 1	9.5 / 2	30.8 / 8
2	14.3 / 5	11.4 / 4	14.3 / 5	17.1 / 6	31.4 / 11	25.7 / 9
3	5.9 / 2	3.3 / 1	26.5 / 9	20.0 / 6	29.3 / 10	36.7 / 11
4	16.0 / 13	12.6 / 11	39.6 / 32	33.3 / 29	18.5 / 15	24.2 / 21

Response
1973 N = 213
1974 N = 216

Reform Score[a]	Decrease Somewhat 1973 (% / No.)	Decrease Somewhat 1974 (% / No.)	Greatly Decrease 1973 (% / No.)	Greatly Decrease 1974 (% / No.)
1	14.3 / 3	34.6 / 9	38.1 / 8	23.1 / 6
2	20.0 / 7	28.7 / 10	20.0 / 7	17.1 / 6
3	26.5 / 9	30.0 / 9	11.8 / 4	10.0 / 3
4	17.3 / 14	23.0 / 20	8.6 / 7	6.9 / 6

[a]For a discussion of the reform scales, see Appendix C.
Note: Percentages computed from number of respondents answering question. Row totals equal 100.0 percent.

characteristics of the respondents' cities and their attitudes on the effect of general revenue sharing. Again, a number of interesting patterns emerge. With only two exceptions (1973 cities in the less than $10,500 category selecting "greatly increase" responses and 1974 cities in the $10,500 to $12,500 category selecting "greatly increase" responses), the higher the income of the city the greater the percentage of respondents indicating a favorable net effect of general revenue-sharing funds on total federal funds. This is no doubt influenced by the greater tendency for lower-income cities to participate in a wider range of categorical grant programs. Thus, revenue sharing was apparently perceived as a substitute for those programs, not as a supplement to them by many of the respondents.

Again, with several exceptions (1974 respondents indicating "increase somewhat" responses in the 5 percent to 15 percent and over 15 percent categories and the 1973 respondents in the 5 percent to 15 percent category indicating the "greatly decrease" response), a clear pattern emerges when non-white population is used. The larger the percentage of non-white population, the greater the attitude that general revenue sharing will have less of a positive and more of a negative effect on total federal funds received. By 1974, 51.7 percent of the respondents in cities with non-white populations exceeding 15 percent felt that the effect of general revenue-sharing funds would be a decrease in total federal funds. Slightly more than 26 percent of the respondents with less than 5 percent non-white populations held that view. It appears that this may be a major reason for the respondents from cities with non-white populations over 15 percent being less favorable towards general revenue sharing. Apparently the furor and turmoil over the demise of the various poverty programs convinced these respondents that general revenue sharing was at best a substitute for these programs and not a net increase in federal funds.

When population change is considered a similar pattern is apparent. As population change increases, the tendency to view general revenue sharing's effect in positive terms also increases. As population change decreases, the tendency to report that general revenue funds will have a negative effect on total federal funds increases. There are minor exceptions in the 1973 over 25 percent ("greatly increase"); 1973, 0 percent to 25 percent ("increase somewhat"); and 1973, 0 percent to 25 percent ("decrease somewhat") categories. This would provide a logical explanation for the previously discussed point that more rapidly growing cities were more favorable in evaluating general revenue sharing than those cities with lesser population change. The conclusion is clear; selected demographic and structural variables are associated with varying attitudes towards the effect of general revenue sharing. These results provide the basis for a consideration of the coalitions that are likely to form during the upcoming legislative process.

Conclusion

Before discussing the various strategies and coalitions that are likely to develop during the legislative renewal struggle, it is important that the prevailing patterns in Tables 6-1 to 6-6 are fully understood. First, respondents were generally quite favorable in their evaluation of general revenue sharing despite the fact that they did not believe general revenue sharing would greatly increase the total amount of federal funds received by their cities. Second, regional variations were most apparent in the Northeast and North Central on the evaluation question and in the Northeast and South on the effect question. Third, governmental structure was associated with differing perceptions of evaluation and effect. Those cities that were less reformed were less favorable towards general revenue sharing and tended to feel the program's effect on total federal funds would be negative. Fourth, and last, demographic variables such as mean income, percent non-white population, and population change were associated with attitudes towards the effect of general revenue sharing. Cities with large non-white populations, lower mean incomes, and little population change were more negative in their estimation of the effect of general revenue sharing funds on total federal funds received. This was a possible major factor in their less consistent evaluation of the general revenue-sharing program.

With these conclusions in mind, a brief discussion of possible city coalitions is in order. To begin, as the responses to the overall satisfaction question indicates, leaders in cities over 50,000 will continue to voice strong approval of general revenue sharing. There will be neither significant nor well-organized opposition to the program from city officials in cities over 50,000, but there will probably be a concerted effort on the part of leaders from some of these cities to alter the formula and distribution procedures as well as to eliminate expenditure restrictions. Cities with substantial public demand for increased services—usually cities with significant low incomes and large non-white populations—will attempt to gain increased allocations based on their needs. Cities that cannot justify increased revenues on need will no doubt favor formulas that will make general revenue-sharing funds more dependent upon population distribution and less so on per capita income and urbanized population.

In similar fashion, cities in general will probably want a larger share of the total revenue-sharing funds to come directly to them rather than the two-thirds of the total funds that do so at the present time. Attitudes on this will vary as the state's use of its general revenue-sharing funds vary. Those states that have used a large proportion of their funds for urban programs will not be criticized as others who have not. In any case, the distribution procedure will be discussed and carefully weighed.

Table 6-8
Effect of General Revenue-Sharing Funds on Total Federal Funds and City Socio-economic Characteristics

Responses 1973 N = 213 1974 N = 216	Greatly Increase				Increase Somewhat				No Effect			
	1973		1974		1973		1974		1973		1974	
	%	No.	%	No.	%	No.	%	No.	%	No.	%	No.
Income												
Less than $10,500	8.1	5	11.1	8	25.8	16	12.5	9	25.8	16	20.8	15
$10,500 to $12,500	9.7	8	7.8	6	34.1	28	28.6	22	22.0	18	32.4	25
Over $12,500	28.9	11	15.9	7	28.9	11	31.8	14	21.1	8	25.0	11
Nonwhite Population												
Less than 5%	19.7	15	19.5	17	28.9	22	26.5	23	32.9	25	27.6	24
5% to 15%	12.5	6	6.4	3	29.1	14	21.3	10	16.7	8	23.4	11
Over 15%	3.5	2	—	—	33.3	19	20.7	12	15.8	9	27.6	16
Population Change												
Less than 0%	5.9	3	3.7	2	27.4	14	13.0	7	25.5	13	16.7	9
0% to 25%	16.9	13	14.1	13	28.5	22	22.8	21	18.2	14	29.4	27
Over 25%	14.8	8	12.8	6	35.2	19	36.2	17	27.8	15	31.9	15

	Decrease Somewhat				Greatly Decrease			
	1973		1974		1973		1974	
Responses 1973 N = 213 1974 N = 216	%	No.	%	No.	%	No.	%	No.
Income								
Less than $10,500	21.0	13	38.9	28	19.3	12	16.7	12
$10,500 to $12,500	18.3	15	20.8	16	15.9	13	10.4	8
Over $12,500	15.8	6	20.5	9	5.3	2	6.8	3
Nonwhite Population								
Less than 5%	10.6	8	16.1	14	7.9	6	10.3	9
5% to 15%	18.8	9	36.1	17	22.9	11	12.8	6
Over 15%	29.8	17	37.9	22	17.6	10	13.8	8
Population Change								
Less than 0%	15.7	8	38.8	21	25.5	13	27.8	15
0% to 25%	24.7	19	26.1	24	11.7	9	7.6	7
Over 25%	13.0	7	17.0	8	9.2	5	2.1	1

Note: Percentages computed from number of respondents answering questions. Row totals equal 100.0 percent.

Finally, larger cities that have more extensive programs will ask that the general revenue-sharing funds take into account both the number of functions performed by a governmental unit and the relative greater need for flexibility on the part of larger cities. For instance, not all cities perform the same range of functions and in many cases there is considerable discrepancy in the range of functions performed.[16] Yet the allocation formula for general revenue-sharing funds does not take this into consideration. Obviously those cities performing a wider range of functions will press for more funds, while those with more restricted funds are likely to maintain that allocations should be based on population alone.

While these legislative provisions will be contended, it is most likely that a coalition of cities comprised of large Northeastern and North Central cities with partisan forms of city government and having significant low incomes and large non-white populations will press for these and other changes that directly affect them. Opposing them, it can be expected that a coalition of suburban, more reform structure city governments with lower non-white and low-income populations, but with higher growth rates will form. The lobbying effort to sway the members of the House and Senate will be most interesting to observe as both coalitions will want legislation increasing their relative and absolute share of the funds but will not want to jeopardize the final chances of the legislation passing.

On a related point, probably just one dominant position will emerge. City leaders will attempt to get a longer authorization and appropriation period for the program than the initial five-year period.[17] The main argument that will be made for this position is that uncertainty about future funding will in fact reduce the innovative use of general revenue-sharing funds. As the discussion in Chapter 5 indicated, cities were not overly innovative or original in their use of general revenue-sharing funds. It will be most interesting to observe the lobbying effort on this aspect of the legislation as any increase in the length of authorization and appropriation strengthens the cities, while a decrease strengthens Congress since it increases Congressional involvement and control.

Speculation about various city coalitions should not ignore the fact that cities are not the only recipients of general revenue-sharing funds nor is the legislative struggle isolated from the general political developments of our time. If the Ford Administration or Congress were to decide that the funding level of general revenue sharing is to stay at the present $6.0+ billion/year, increases in the amounts received by cities would have to come from the amounts received by other jurisdictions. Since states, counties, and townships are the principal other recipients, the next legislative process may be marked by extensive in-fighting by spokesmen for these different jurisdictions. Even more likely is the possibility that coalitions will form that cut across jurisdictional lines and reflect underlying common characteristics. For instance, it would be logical for urban counties to work with larger urban centers to increase the impact urbanization has on the allocation formula of general revenue-sharing funds. In similar fashion, more rural counties might work with the smaller cities and suburbs for the continued and even increased role of income in the formula.

Two aspects of coalition development are interesting. The first involves the role the states will play in the lobbying and legislative effort. Will they simply attempt to maintain their present role or will they seek greater amounts of funds? Also, will the states act and speak as a unit or will the more populous, urbanized, and economically better-off clash with the more rural, sparsely populated, and less economic bountiful states. Obviously the stakes are high for state governments and they have a vital interest in the legislative outcomes.

A second aspect of the coalition politics is the role the townships will play in the legislative process. Often cited as performing little real function in some areas, their proportion of general revenue-sharing funds could be severely threatened. Will the township leaders permit this to happen or will they enter the political fray?

Certainly one of the oldest bromides in America, "politics makes strange bedfellows," will be proved by the upcoming legislative debate. If the 1974 elections result in the election of more than the usual urban and more liberal members to the House of Representatives, then the city leaders wanting more favorable provisions for low-income and densely populated areas may prevail. If the elections are indecisive, the lobbying efforts mounted by the various groups will be instrumental in determining the legislative outcomes. In any case, the legislative process will provide a most interesting setting for political lobbying and finally the resolution of the policy matters under consideration. Given these various environmental and political factors, what is the future of general revenue sharing and what importance does it have for those interested in the study or urban politics and political decentralization? These questions are considered in the concluding chapter.

Notes

1. See Public Law 92-512, Section 105 (b), for a discussion of the initial funding of general revenue sharing.

2. See Public Law 92-512, Section 106, for the "three" and "five" factor formulae that give appropriate weight to population, urbanization, tax effort, income tax collections, and per capita income.

3. See Public Law 92-512, Sections 107 and 108, for a complete de-

scription of the various governmental units entitled to receive general revenue sharing funds.

4. See Public Law 92-512, Sections 103, 104, and 121-123, for a discussion of those restrictions.

5. See Public Law 92-512, Subtitle B Administrative Requirements, for a discussion of these points.

6. There has been considerable discussion over this point. For a variety of views see Austin B. Williams, *Revenue Sharing and the Black Community* (New York: National Urban League, 1973); National Council on the Aging, *Revenue Sharing and the Elderly: How to Play and Win* (Washington: National Council on the Aging, 1974); and Office of Revenue Sharing, *Getting Involved—Your Guide to General Revenue Sharing* (Washington: Office of Revenue Sharing, 1974).

7. Moon Landrieu, Statement to the Senate Government Operat..ns Subcommittee on Intergovernmental Relations, June 11, 1974, p. 15. We would like to thank Stephen T. Honey, Counsel, Office of Federal Relations of the National League of Cities and United States Conference of Mayors, for providing us with a copy of the statement.

8. Comments were broadcast during a *Meet the Press* broadcast at the June 1974 meeting of the Conference of Mayors.

9. See *1973 Congressional Quarterly Almanac* for a discussion of these proposals.

10. Landrieu, p. 17.

11. Ibid., p. 12.

12. The points discussed in Chapter 1 are appropriate here. Can citizen groups muster the necessary political strength to influence specific and pending legislation when their position is opposed by other groups?

13. Perhaps the most interesting discussion of political tides is found in Richard M. Scammon and Ban J. Wattenberg, *The Real Majority* (New York: Coward, McCann and Geohegan, Inc., 1970), pp. 25-34.

14. Landrieu, p. 1.

15. See then concluding comments in Raymond E. Wolfinger and John Osgood Field, "Political Ethos and the Structure of City Government," *The American Political Science Review*, LX (June 1966) pp. 324-6.

16. For insightful comments concerning the functions and roles of various city governments, see the comments attributed to John Parker, Deputy Director, Office of Revenue Sharing, by Martin Tolchin, "Behind Revenue Sharing," *The New York Times*, June 29, 1974, p. 34.

17. Landrieu, pp. 3 and 18.

7

**General Revenue Sharing:
The New American
Revolution?**

Introduction

This book has examined in considerable detail the fiscal and political impacts of general revenue sharing on urban America. In this concluding chapter, we attempt to summarize our substantive findings, discuss their theoretical implications, and arrive at tentative judgments concerning the relative merits of general revenue sharing.

Empirical Findings

One of the most important findings of this study is that American cities are allocating general revenue sharing funds in a relatively few program areas. Thus, in 1973 it was found that the five areas of law enforcement, fire prevention, environmental protection, street and road repair, and parks and recreation received over 53 percent of general revenue-sharing funds. In 1974, the proportion alloted to these areas was over 68 percent. Our findings in this regard parallel very closely those reported in official Office of Revenue Sharing publications.

Although the cities in our study are most accurately described in terms of their uniformity in revenue-sharing spending, some interesting, if often minor, deviations were noted. Of those factors associated with differing expenditure patterns, region, population growth, and governmental structure appear to be the most significant. We find that the South especially deviates in its revenue-sharing expenditure patterns. Whereas the other regions all allocated over 30 percent or more of their funds to public safety functions in 1974 (the Northeast allocated 54 percent), the Southern cities allocated only about 13 percent of their funds for this function. Also, we find noticeable expenditure differences when "controlling for" form of government. Mayor-council cities have been more likely to spend their funds for public safety; council-manager cities have spent larger proportions of general revenue-sharing funds for street and road repair and parks and recreation. Likewise, population change appears to have affected revenue-sharing allocations. Cities losing population are more likely to have allocated general revenue-sharing funds to public safety functions than those cities gaining population more rapidly.

147

When examining the program *consequences* of revenue-sharing expenditures, even more pronounced differences among the cities were observed. While most of the cities report spending general revenue-sharing funds for existing programs, an examination of expenditures by functional categories revealed rather dramatic distinctions. Thus, over 75 percent of those funds spent for law enforcement and fire prevention have been allocated to existing programs, very nearly half of the funds allocated to social services has been used to support new programs. Other functional areas in which substantial proportions of general revenue-sharing funds have been used to fund new programs include health, parks and recreation, libraries, and transit systems. Thus, while the overall conclusion is that the majority of general revenue-sharing money has been used to bolster existing and on-going programs, it is also true that in some functional areas substantial proportions of the funds have been used for new and innovative programs. We suggest, then, that the "popular" assumption that revenue-sharing funds are being used to maintain existing programs is accurate but that this must be modified to account for a considerable amount of innovation in selected functional areas.

Also, it was found that most of the responding officials believe that revenue sharing has been responsible for the prevention of taxing increases in their cities, and that the less wealthy, larger central cities were more likely to so respond. It was also found that about 40 percent of the responding officials believed that general revenue sharing will result in a net decrease in the amount of funds received by their cities, and officials in the less wealthy, larger central cities were more likely to so respond.

In general, our findings concerning the allocation and impact of revenue-sharing funds can be summarized in the following table. This table indicates that both in the allocation of general revenue-sharing funds and in the program's reported impact on urban areas, two broad patterns are evident. While we do not mean to imply that the patterns noted in this table are necessarily representative of any single city displaying these characteristics, the overall conclusion is that non-Southern, mayor cities, and those losing population have allocated their general revenue-sharing funds differently from Southern (and to some extent, Western), manager-run cities that are gaining in population. In general, cities in the first-mentioned category are more likely to have spent their funds for public safety functions and for social services; cities in the second category are more likely to have spent their funds on environmental concerns, street and road repair, and for parks and recreation.

Likewise, it is found that the *impact* of revenue sharing can be discussed in terms of two broad categories of cities. The less wealthy, larger, central cities are more likely to have spent their general revenue-sharing funds for existing programs; to indicate they will use the funds for OEO and

Table 7-1

Expenditure and Impact Consequences of General Revenue Sharing: A Summary Table

Expenditure Decision:[a]	Categories of Cities	
	Mayor-Council Losing Population Non-Southern	Council-Manager Increasing Population Southern (Western)
Law Enforcement	+	−
Fire Prevention	+	−
Social Services	+	−
Health Functions	+	−
Environment	−	+
Street and Road Repair	−	+
Parks and Recreation	−	+

Impact:	Categories of Cities	
	Less Wealthy Larger Central Cities	More Wealthy Smaller Suburban Cities
Use of Funds	Existing Programs	New Programs
Citizen Participation	Yes	No
Support of OEO and Model Cities	Yes	No
Impact on Taxing Levels	Lowered or Maintained	No Effect
Impact on Receipt of Federal Funds	Decrease	Increase

[a]The "+" symbol means that for the most part, cities displaying the characteristic allocated a larger proportion of revenue-sharing funds to the category examined than the average; "−" indicates that most of the cities allocated less than the average for that function.

Note: It should be clear that this table represents overall trends and is not meant to be indicative of the spending or impact patterns of any single city.

Model Cities programs, if necessary; to report general revenue sharing as responsible for the lowering of tax rates (or at least maintaining stability); to have encouraged the participation of citizens in the allocation of general revenue-sharing funds; and to believe that general revenue sharing will mean a net decrease in amounts of federal funds received.

Thus, although we must caution the reader again that many of these distinctions are not major, we do find noticeable differences in both the expenditure and impact of general revenue sharing among two broad categories of cities. This again supports our conclusion discussed in Chapter 6 that, in future revenue-sharing debates, spokesmen for American cities might be expected to coalesce into two groups. Each group, we believe, will be in favor of continuing and even expanding general revenue-sharing funds; however, their specific proposals for alterations in the distribution formula may dramatically clash. The implications of this

for the future of the revenue-sharing legislation are discussed in the concluding section of this chapter.

Theoretical Interests

As discussed above, the study of general revenue-sharing expenditures
presents several interesting theoretical questions for scholars of municipal
politics. Such a study, we have argued, provides an opportunity to explore
important theoretical issues in the following areas: the relationship between structural and environmental factors in policy decisions, policy
innovation, citizen participation in municipal affairs and the impact of such
participation on policy outcomes, and federalism. Throughout this book,
these have been discussed; here, the important points are very briefly
summarized.

In the first place, it was noted that revenue-sharing expenditures offer
an opportunity to re-examine one of the paramount concerns of policy
analysts: the relationship between environmental influences, political factors, and policy decisions. We did find evidence to indicate that form of
government appears to be associated with differing general revenue-
sharing decisions; however, as is true of most recent policy studies, the
most important factors in this regard appear to be environmental. In this
instance, region of the country and population change appear to be the most
important factors associated with differing revenue-sharing decisions.

Concerning policy innovation and the speed with which cities are able
to reach decisions concerning the allocation of new infusions of funds, our
findings lend support to those who have found that centralized political
structures facilitate policy innovation. Again, however, it is noted that
these distinctions may be largely accounted for by environmental factors.

Citizen participation and its impact on decision making is an especially
interesting topic to examine from the revenue-sharing perspective. As
mentioned above, general revenue sharing differs from other major
federal-local grant-in-aid programs in that general revenue sharing requires
no participation of citizens prior to the expenditure of those funds. Yet, it is
found that about half of the cities responding to our survey had allowed or
encouraged some degree of citizen input. This may provide evidence to
support the conclusion that one of the most important consequences of the
OEO and Model Cities programs has been the establishment of both the
precedent and tradition of citizen involvement in municipal decision making. Just as important, we find that, at least concerning the expenditure of
general revenue-sharing funds, such participation may make a difference.
Thus, it was found that cities *not* holding public hearings were much more
likely to spend their general revenue-sharing funds for public safety func-

tions; those allowing some degree of citizen participation were more likely to evenly distribute their funds and spent larger proportions in such areas as steeet and road repair, parks and recreation, direct tax relief, social services, and health services. We realize that our data do not allow a "causal" interpretation of these findings; however, it can be said that citizen participation is associated with different patterns of general revenue-sharing expenditures.

Another interesting aspect of general revenue sharing concerns the bureaucratic apparatus established to administer the program. An often-heard criticism of the categorical grant programs was that so much money and energy was expended on administrative functions that little remained for distribution to those for whom the program was intended to benefit. Although our study was not designed specifically to deal with this aspect, a statement recently issued by Graham Watt, Director of the Office of Revenue Sharing, does raise this point.[1] As indicated in that statement, the Office of Revenue Sharing as of June 1, 1974, was comprised of a total of 68 employees and projects an expansion to 121 by June 30, 1975.[2] Watt indicated in that statement that the total projected cost of implementing general revenue sharing in Fiscal Year 1975 to represent only 13/100s of 1 percent of the total funds to be distributed in that year.[3] Clearly, the bureaucratic growth and administrative cost associated with previous programs funded at similar levels have not occurred with general revenue sharing.

Related to the question of bureaucratic size is the issue of administrative efficiency—that is, can a program administered by such a small staff supply the technical advice and compliance oversight necessary for efficient and proper dispersion of such a large amount of funds? Our findings indicate, as reported in Chapter 6, that those cities included in our survey are overwhelmingly satisfied with the administration of general revenue sharing to date and that this satisfaction is increasing. In his statement, Director Watt indicated the status of compliance complaints handled by the Office of Revenue Sharing. Table 7-2 presents that information.

As indicated, by June 1974, the Office of Revenue Sharing has handled some 92 complaints (an additional 40 were found to be unrelated to revenue-sharing expenditures). Of the 92 complaints, 45 have been resolved to the satisfaction of all parties; 46 are in various stages of investigation; and 1 has been referred to the Department of Justice for civil action. While this would appear to be an enviable record, it is noted that in Watt's statement that he has requested a substantial increase in the number of employees assigned to the compliance division of the Office of Revenue Sharing by June 1975. Table 7-3 indicates the projected growth in all divisions of the Office of Revenue Sharing by June 1975.

As civil rights and other groups representing minority interests continue

Table 7-2
Complaints Handled by the Office of Revenue Sharing (As of June 1, 1974)

		Status		
Nature of Complaints	Resolved	In Process	In Court	Total
Civil Rights/Discrimination	18	22	1	41
Financial/Accounting	5	4	0	9
Legal Compliance	11	11	0	22
Miscellaneous	11	9	0	20
TOTAL	45	46	1	92

Source: Table 8, Statement of Graham W. Watt, Director of the Office of Revenue Sharing before the Intergovernmental Relations Subcommittee of the Senate Committee on Government Operations (Washington, D.C., June 4, 1974), p. 35.

Table 7-3
Office of Revenue-Sharing Employment

Division	Actual 6/1/74	Proposed 6/30/75
Office of the Director	5	5
Administration	4	5
Program Planning and Coordination	2	3
Public Affairs	2	3
Data and Demography	7	9
Intergovernmental Relations	12	17
Systems and Operations	17	28
Compliance	19	51
TOTALS	68	121

Source: Table, Statement of Graham W. Watt, Director of the Office of Revenue Sharing before the Intergovernmental Relations Subcommittee of the Senate Committee on Government Operations (Washington, D.C., June 4, 1974), Table 9, p. 43.

to become involved in local decision making, a larger number of compliance complaints may be forthcoming. It would be most interesting to compare the incidence of non-compliance with general revenue sharing provisions with that experienced in programs with greater compliance requirements. Such a comparison would be necessary for a truly objective determination of the ability of ORS to successfully resolve compliance issues.

Of course, the most important theoretical question addressed by our research concerns the impact of decentralized decision making. As has been discussed throughout, traditional theories of American federalism would argue that broader decision-making arenas are more redistributive in nature; narrower decision-making arenas are expected to result in more conservative and status quo policies. General revenue sharing, with its emphasis on decentralized decision making, has provided an ideal opportunity to test this assumption. We do find, as most theories of federalism suggest, that the allocation of general revenue-sharing funds must be described as largely conservative and status quo oriented. As stressed throughout, such functional areas as law enforcement and fire prevention are receiving the bulk of general revenue-sharing funds; such areas as health and social services are receiving relatively small proportions. To this extent, we find that traditional theories of federalism apply.

At the same time, it was found that cities allowing some degree of citizen participation are spending their funds in a more redistributive fashion (i.e., less money for public safety and more for social services, health, and other amenities). While these differences are not large, there is some evidence to suggest that citizen organizations may to some extent reverse the expected results of decentralized decision making. The most important legacy of the OEO, Model Cities, and urban renewal programs of the 1960s, we would suggest, may not be whether or not they succeeded in eliminating slums or poverty, but that they encouraged the organization and politization of those at the local level previously ignored in the decision-making process. The results of this organization, we believe, are reflected in differing patterns of revenue-sharing expenditures as reported above. E. E. Schattschneider's observation that "probably almost 90 percent of the people cannot get into the pressure system"[4] may be less applicable today than when he made his comments in 1960, prior to OEO and Model Cities. Organization of socially oriented groups at the local level, we suggest, can to some degree neutralize the traditionally conservative orientation of decentralized decision making. Of course the "openness" of the local political system to citizen input will be quite important in determining the final impact the input will have. Local groups, if they wish to maximize their chances for success, need to develop political organizations and strategies that maximize their impact on local decision makers. In many cases this may take considerable time and, in some cases, it may well be impossible. To the extent that local groups and groups formally not interested in or prevented from participating and affecting local budgetary decision making achieve success, revisions of the traditional theories of American federalism are in order.

General Revenue Sharing: Evaluation and Assessment

Finally, we come to the most difficult questions of this study: Is general revenue sharing working, should it be continued, how should it be altered? Our judgments in these areas, it must be stressed, are necessarily highly tentative. In the first place, our data were collected at the half-way point of the program. It is conceivable (although we believe highly unlikely) that expenditure and impact trends reported above may be altered as the remainder of the funds are allocated and disbursed. Secondly, it is recalled that ours is a study of cities over 50,000. Although these cities receive the bulk of those funds disbursed to urban areas, our findings are not necessarily applicable to smaller cities and certainly not to other governmental jurisdictions. In addition, as we have stressed throughout, a final evaluation of general revenue sharing will be possible only when considering the results of several studies employing a variety of research methodologies and perspectives. Because of its nature, the impact of general revenue sharing is very much a subjective evaluation, and all viewpoints must be considered prior to a final judgment.

In spite of these limitations and reservations, we believe that our findings support a number of important assessments. First, general revenue sharing obviously has not been responsible for bold, new, and innovative programs at the local level. Although we found that in some areas (such as social services) a larger porportion of general revenue-sharing funds have been spent for innovative programs than in others, for the most part general revenue-sharing funds have been used to support on-going programs. At the same time, we find no evidence to support the conclusion that there have occurred gross inefficiencies or wastefulness in revenue-sharing expenditures. Instead, cities appear to be spending their funds in very close proportion to their "normal" (i.e., before revenue sharing) budgetary allocations.

Concerning general revenue sharing's impact on local property taxing levels, it seems clear that the findings are less ambiguous: general revenue sharing has had an immediate and wide-spread effect on reducing or preventing increases in taxing levels. Thus, we find that almost two-thirds of the officials report that general revenue sharing has resulted in the lowering of taxing rates or in the prevention of increases in such taxes. Furthermore, it is found that an even greater proportion of officials believe that the long-range effect of general revenue sharing on taxing rates will be positive. This would indicate that general revenue-sharing funds helped alleviate the fiscal crisis for a substantial number of cities.

No major administrative problems with general revenue sharing are apparent at this point. Certainly our study shows that the vast majority of responding officials are satisfied with the program and that their numbers are increasing. We find the compliance data supplied by Director Watt supportive of this position. For a program disbursing over $30 billion to over 38,000 units of government to have received only 132 complaints (40 of which were found to be unrelated to general revenue-sharing funds) seems to us to be very satisfactory. Of course, as mentioned above, it will be important to continue to follow the nature and quantity of complaints and their resolution throughout the life of the program.

Perhaps the major reservation that we find in the revenue-sharing program concerns the extremely small proportion of funds having been allocated to social service needs. As mentioned throughout, this was not an unexpected finding—localized decision making traditionally has been less redistributive than national decision making. Even this conclusion, however, is modified by two points. First, even though the proportion of general revenue-sharing funds allocated to social service functions is small, the amount does represent on the average more than these same cities allocated to social services in their pre-revenue sharing budget, and this trend seems to be increasing. Also, it was found that those cities allowing citizen input during revenue-sharing decisions spent an even larger proportion of their funds for social services. Thus, the conclusion is clear: groups seeking larger allocations of general revenue-sharing funds for social service functions must organize and compete with other—often more established—groups at the municipal level. Such organization and competition, will of course be difficult, but our findings indicate that it may be productive.

We believe our findings also have important implications concerning possible alterations in the revenue-sharing legislation. It will be recalled that it was found that the expenditure and impact of general revenue sharing differs largely in terms of two broad classifications of cities. Less wealthy, larger, non-Southern, central cities, and those losing population have found it necessary to allocate their general revenue-sharing funds for on-going programs and programs largely in the areas of police protection and fire prevention. Thus, these cities have had to use revenue sharing simply to maintain existing levels of services. It might be argued, then, that revenue-sharing funds are spread too "thinly" among the various units of government and that the money allocated to more wealthy, smaller, suburban cities could more usefully be distributed among larger, central cities —those facing more critical fiscal needs. However severe may be the fiscal need of large central cities, we cannot support such a conclusion. The smaller, suburban cities, it should be pointed out, are those that are allocating their funds much as supporters of general revenue sharing had hoped. Thus, it is these cities that are spending larger proportions of funds for new and innovative functions. In considering possible changes in the general revenue-sharing legislation, then, we believe the data support a change in the distribution giving even more weight than is presently found to the factor of "need." This could be done by giving more weight to the income components in the distribution formula, by reducing the amounts available to other governmental jurisdictions, or by specifying additional funds for the cities based on "need." However, we cannot support attempts to eliminate the smaller, more wealthy jurisdictions, at least of the size category included in this study, as recipients of general revenue-sharing funds. Thus, our conclusion is that general revenue sharing, with the reservations noted above, is working at least as well as previous federal grant programs, and our major policy recommentation would be the continuation (and perhaps extension) of the program, but with alterations in the distribution formula that would weigh more heavily those factors of need.

General revenue sharing, in summary, has not been and will not be a panacea for all the "ills" of urban America. Many of America's most pressing urban problems—such as continuing racial and economic segregation, increasing structural fragmentation, and rising levels of alienation—are largely beyond the pale of almost any fiscal solution. Certainly, general revenue sharing will not solve problems such as these. At the same time, we do find that the program succeeds remarkably well in a number of crucial areas. It apparently is responsible for reducing or maintaining stable property tax rates for a large number of cities; at least some of the funds in some functional areas have been used for new and innovative programs; city officials certainly are united in their approval of the program; and few major administrative problems are evident. These "positive" attributes must be weighed against what we find to be the major deficiency in the program: the reluctance or inability of cities to spend large proportions of the funds for new and socially oriented programs. However, it is our belief that a change in the distribution formula that would increase the proportion of funds allocated to less wealthy, larger, central cities may result in larger proportions of general revenue-sharing funds being spent in new program areas. Likewise, we find evidence to support the conclusion that those groups interested in having greater proportions of general revenue-sharing money allocated to social services can be successful by organizing and competing at the local level.

In the final analysis, this may well be the most important contribution of general revenue sharing: the stimulation of citizen interest in local politics and the encouragement of increased and more effective participation in the urban decision-making process by previously ignored and uninvolved groups. If revenue sharing does serve as such a catalyst, former President Nixon's often-quoted prediction that revenue sharing marks a new American revolution, one designed to return power to the people, may yet prove accurate.

Notes

1. Graham W. Watt, *Statement Before the Intergovernmental Rela-*

tions Subcommittee of the Senate Committee on Government Operations (Washington, D.C.: Office of Revenue Sharing, June 4, 1974).

    2. Ibid., p. 43.

    3. Ibid., p. 45.

    4. E. E. Schattschneider, *The Semi-Sovereign People* (New York: Holt, Rinehart and Winston, 1960), p. 35.

Appendixes

Appendix A
Research Strategy and Questionnaires

Our research began after a series of conversations in September 1972, when it became obvious that Congress was going to pass the State and Local Fiscal Assistance Act of 1972 and that former President Nixon would sign it. We decided not to seek initial outside support since the inevitable delay would have hampered the research. The research has been financed from personal sources and various small grants from both George Washington University and Purdue University. The initial survey was mailed in January 1973, and the second one, in January 1974. We expect to continue the research at least through 1976 and possibly longer. Each respondent was sent an explanatory letter and a questionnaire along with a stamped return envelope. Respondents were promised confidentiality; hence, we do not discuss specific cities in our analysis. Respondents were also asked to indicate whether they wanted a copy of the questionnaire results; in both years, over 95 percent of the respondents indicated they did. We believe this procedure helped increase our return rate. In May of 1973 and 1974, all the respondents were sent summary results. The change in the 1974 questionnaire was done to make it similar to the actual use reports required by the Office of Revenue Sharing in order to facilitate the respondents' completion. The explanatory letter and questionnaires follow.

1973 Explanatory Letter

We are conducting a study of the initial impact of *Revenue Sharing* (Public Law 92-512) on municipal government and services and would appreciate your assistance in our effort. Would you please provide us with some basic information about the impact of revenue sharing on your community by completing the enclosed questionnaire. The survey is purposefully brief so that it should take less than 5 minutes to complete.

Although the survey is brief, we believe it will provide information of interest to all those concerned with and affected by the revenue-sharing legislation, and we will be pleased to return a summary copy of the results to you if you desire. At the same time, we want to assure you that your responses will remain absolutely confidential and will be used only by us in our comparative study of cities throughout the United States.

Thank you very much for your assistance and we are looking forward to your response.

1973 Revenue-Sharing Survey Questionnaire

Most of the following questions can be answered by placing an (X) or a check after the appropriate response. If you wish to extend your comments, or if you want to discuss an aspect of revenue sharing not covered in the survey, please feel free to use the back of the page for that purpose. All responses are confidential.

1. Approximate what proportion of the revenue-sharing funds received to date by your city have been designated for (road repair, tax relief, etc.)? Less Than 25% _____; 25-50% _____; 50-75% _____; Over 75% _____.

2. Please indicate how revenue-sharing money is to be spent in your city by indicating the approximate *proportion* of total revenue-sharing funds allocated to those functions listed below (Law Enforcement—25%; Fire Prevention—10%, etc.). If your city is to use a proportion of its funds for activities not listed, please indicate that activity and the proportion it is to receive in the space* provided.

Expenditure for: *Proportion of Total Revenue-Sharing Funds:*

(1) Law Enforcement--- _____ %

(2) Fire Prevention --- _____ %

(3) Building and Zoning Code Enforcement -------------------- _____ %

(4) Environmental Protection (sewage, pollution,

   sanitation, etc.) --- _____ %

(5) Transit Systems --- _____ %

(6) Street and Road Repair ------------------------------------- _____ %

(7) Social Services (for the poor, aged, and

   minority groups)--- _____ %

(8) Health Services-- _____ %

(9) Recreation and Parks -- _____ %

(10) Public Building Renovation ------------------------------------ _____ %

(11) Supplementing Municipal Salaries ---------------------------- _____ %

(12) Tax Relief-- _____ %

(13) Investments-- _____ %

(14) Previous Debt Retirement --- ____ %

(15) Capital Expenditures (please specify) ------------------------- ____ %

(16) *Other (please specify) -- ____ %

(17) *Other (please specify) -- ____ %

(18) Undetermined --- ____ %

Total: 100 %

3. In attempting to determine how revenue-sharing funds are to be spent, has your city encouraged (or does it plan to encourage) neighborhood or community-wide "hearings" where citizen opinions could be expressed? Yes____; No____.

4. Do you expect your city to hold periodic public hearings as future revenue-sharing checks are issued? Yes____; No____; Undecided____.

5. If your community now is receiving Model Cities, Urban Renewal, or Office of Economic Opportunity (OEO) funds, do you believe your city will allocate a portion of its future revenue-sharing funds to those activities should these programs not be renewed by the U.S. Congress as President Nixon has requested? Definitely Yes ____; Probably Yes ____; Uncertain ____; Probably Not ____; Definitely Not ____.

6. Has your city assigned (or does it intend to assign) personnel to devote *full-time* attention exclusively to revenue-sharing matters? If so, how many? None ____; One ____; More than one (please specify how many) ____.

7. Would you say that revenue-sharing funds received to date by your city have been used (or will be used) mainly to supplement, improve, or extend *existing* services or have they been used (or will be used) mainly to fund *new* programs? Used mainly to supplement *existing* programs ____; Used mainly to fund *new* programs ____.

8. As you know, some local officials believe that, even with revenue sharing, the *total* amount of funds received annually from the federal government by their city will *decrease* if programs such as Model Cities and OEO are reduced or eliminated. How about your city—what do you believe will be the actual long-run effect of the revenue-sharing concept on federal funds received by *your* community? Greatly Increase ____; Increase Somewhat ____; Little or No Effect ____; Decrease Somewhat ____; Greatly Decrease ____.

9. Finally, we are interested in your overall *evaluation* of the concept of

revenue sharing and its implications for your community at this early stage of the program. In general, would you say that to date you are very pleased with the revenue-sharing program, somewhat pleased, or what? Very Satisfied _____; Somewhat Satisfied _____; Undecided _____; Somewhat Unsatisfied _____; Very Unsatisfied _____.

10. Do you wish to receive a summary copy of the results of this study? Yes _____; No _____.

1974 Explanatory Letter

We are continuing our study of the impact of *Revenue Sharing* (Public Law 92-512) on municipal government and services and would appreciate your assistance in our effort. Would you please provide us with some basic information about the revenue-sharing decisions reached in your community by completing the enclosed questionnaire. All questions pertain to the planned or actual use of general revenue-sharing funds for the present fiscal year (Entitlement Period 4), July 1, 1973 to June 30, 1974. The survey is purposefully brief so that it should take less than 5 minutes to complete.

Although the survey is brief, we believe it will provide information of interest to all those concerned with and affected by the revenue-sharing legislation, and we will be pleased to return a summary copy of the results to you if you desire. At the same time, we want to assure you that your responses will remain absolutely confidential and will be used only by us in our comparative study of cities throughout the United States.

Thank you very much for your assistance and we are looking forward to your response.

1974 Revenue-Sharing Survey Questionnaire

Most of the following questions can be answered by placing an (X) or a check after the appropriate response. If you wish to extend your comments, or if you want to discuss an aspect of revenue sharing not covered in the survey, please feel free to use the back of the page for that purpose. All responses are confidential.

1. Please indicate how the revenue-sharing funds for the present fiscal year (Entitlement Period 4) are to be spent in your city by indicating the approximate *proportion* of total revenue-sharing funds allocated to those functions listed below (Law Enforcement—25%; Fire Prevention—10%, etc.). If your city is to use a proportion of its funds for activities not listed, please indicate that activity and the proportion it is to receive in the space* provided.

	Proportion of Total Revenue-Sharing Funds:		To Be Used Mainly For (Please check one)	
	Operating	Capital	Supplementing Existing Programs	Funding New Programs
(1) Law Enforcement	____ %	____ %	_____ or	_____
(2) Fire Prevention	____ %	____ %	_____ or	_____
(3) Building and Zoning Code Enforcement	____ %	____ %	_____ or	_____
(4) Environmental Protection (sewage, pollution, sanitation, etc.)	____ %	____ %	_____ or	_____
(5) Transit Systems	____ %	____ %	_____ or	_____
(6) Street and Road Repair	____ %	____ %	_____ or	_____
(7) Social Services (for the poor, aged, and minority groups)	____ %	____ %	_____ or	_____

(8) Health Services ———————— % ———— % or ————————

(9) Recreation and Parks ———————— % ———— % or ————————

(10) Public Building Renovation ———————— % ———— % or ————————

(11) Supplementing Municipal Salaries ———————— % ———— % or ————————

(12) Tax Relief ———————— % ———— % or ————————

(13) Investments ———————— % ———— % or ————————

(14) Previous Debt Retirement ———————— % ———— % or ————————

(15) Libraries ———————— % ———— % or ————————

(16) Financial Administration ———————— % ———— % or ————————

(17) *Other (please specify) ———————— % ———— % or ————————

(18) Undetermined ———————— % ———— % or ————————

Total = 100 %

2. In attempting to determine how this fiscal year's revenue-sharing funds are to be spent, has your city encouraged (or does it plan to encourage) neighborhood or community-wide "hearings" where citizen opinions could be expressed? Yes _____; No _____.

3. Do you expect your city to hold periodic public hearings as future revenue-sharing checks are issued? Yes _____; No _____.

4. If your community now is receiving Model Cities, Urban Renewal, or Office of Economic Opportunity (OEO) funds, do you believe your city will allocate a portion of this fiscal year's or future revenue-sharing funds to those activities should these programs not be renewed by the U.S. Congress as President Nixon has requested? Definitely Yes _____; Probably Yes _____; Uncertain _____; Probably Not _____; Definitely Not _____.

5. Has your city assigned (or does it intend to assign) personnel to devote *full-time* attention exclusively to revenue-sharing matters? If so, how many? None _____; One _____; More than one (please specify how many) _____.

6. As you know, some local officials believe that, even with revenue sharing, the *total* amount of funds received annually from the federal government by their city will *decrease* if programs such as Model Cities and OEO are reduced or eliminated. How about your city—what do you believe will be the actual long-run effect of the revenue-sharing concept on federal funds received by *your* community? Greatly Increase _____; Increase Somewhat _____; Little or No Effect _____; Decrease Somewhat _____; Greatly Decrease _____.

7. Compared with previous years, how has your city's tax rate changed this fiscal year? Greatly Increased _____; Increased Somewhat _____; Little or No Change _____; Decreased Somewhat _____; Greatly Decreased _____.

8. What effect, if any, did the receipt of general revenue-sharing funds have on this year's tax rate? Allowed for a reduction in tax rate _____; Prevented increase in tax rate _____; Reduced amount of rate increase in tax _____; No effect on tax rate _____.

9. Assuming general revenue-sharing funds continue at their present rate through the remaining years covered by the act, what do you believe will be the long-range effect of general revenue sharing on the tax rate of your city? Will allow for a reduction in tax rate _____; Will prevent increases in tax rate _____; Will reduce amount of rate increase in tax _____; Will have no effect on tax rate _____.

10. Finally, we are interested in your overall *evaluation* of the concept of revenue sharing and its implications for your community at this early stage of the program. In general, would you say that to date you are

very pleased with the revenue-sharing program, somewhat pleased, or what? Very Satisfied _____; Somewhat Satisfied _____; Undecided _____; Somewhat Unsatisfied _____; Very Unsatisfied _____.

11. Do you wish to receive a summary copy of the results of this study? Yes _____.

Appendix B
Restrictions on Expenditure of General Revenue Sharing Funds

States and local units of government are prohibited from using their general revenue sharing funds:

1. As matching funds for federal grant-in-aid programs;
2. For any project or program discriminating on the basis of race, color, national origin, or sex;
3. For projects or programs violating the Davis-Bacon labor act.

In addition, states and local units of government are required to:

1. Establish a separate trust fund for general revenue-sharing funds received.
2. Publish both planned use reports prior to each entitlement period and actual use reports at the end of each entitlement period;
3. Submit the planned and actual use reports to the Office of Revenue Sharing;
4. Provide additional information or audit capabilities as required.

States may spend their general revenue-sharing funds without restrictions; local units of government must spend their funds for "priority expenditure" and "ordinary and necessary" capital expenditures. The following uses indicate the priority expenditure categories and the various ways general revenue-sharing funds may be allocated within them:

Category[a]	Expenditure
1. Public Safety	Preservation of law and order, traffic safety, vehicular inspection, detention and custody of persons awaiting trial, crime prevention activities, and parole activities. Fire fighting organization, fire prevention, fire hazard inspection, fire hydrants, and equipment.
2. Environmental Protection/ Conservation	Restoration and protection of the environment including soil, water and air conservation. Sanitation services such as garbage collection and disposal, public incinerators. Sewerage disposal including lines, laboratories, and disposal stations.

[a]Source: David A. Caputo and Richard L. Cole, *Revenue Sharing: The First Actual Use Reports* (Washington, D.C.: The Office of Revenue Sharing, 1974), pp. 44-45.

3. Public Transportation	Mass transit systems, highways, bridges, ferries, tunnels, airports, streetlights, traffic lights and traffic signs.
4. Health/Hospitals	Hospital facilities such as buildings, beds, supplies. Health services such as research, clinics, nursing, and general public health.
5. Recreation/Culture	Parks, boating and camping facilities, recreational and sport programs. Cultural planning, museums, and orchestras.
6. Libraries	Public libraries, books, maps, census information, special collections.
7. Social Services for the Poor or Aged	Welfare institutions, categorical public assistance programs, public welfare vendor payments for health and/or services based on need.
8. Financial Administration	Offices and agencies concerned with tax assessment and collection, central accounting, disbursement of funds, debt management, supervision of financial administration.

Appendix C
Reform Scale

As the discussion in Chapter 1 indicated, there has been considerable scholarly interest and discussion concerning the impact of government structure on policy outcomes and decision making. We decided to incorporate a reform scale throughout the analysis to investigate the impact political structure had on general revenue-sharing decision making.

Each of the respondents had their city's form of government, method of council election (at-large or district), and municipal ballot type (partisan or non-partisan) coded. The *Municipal Year Book* was the source for this data. Listed below are the various characteristics.

Characteristic:	Reform:	Non-Reform:
Form of Government	Council-Manager Commission	Mayor-Council
Council Election	At-Large	District
Ballot Type	Non-Partisan	Partisan

A city received a 1 each time it had a reform characteristic and a 0 when it did not. Thus, reform scores ranged from 0 (least reformed) to 3 (most reformed). For analysis and reporting purposes, the scores were changed to 1 (least reformed) and 4 (most reformed). The 1 to 4 scale is used throughout this book. In this respect, the scale of reformism employed in this study is similar to that constructed and used by Robert L. Lineberry and Edmund P. Fowler, "Reformism and Public Policies in American Cities," *The American Political Science Review* LXI (September 1967), pp. 701-16.

Indexes

Author Index

Ashley, Thomas, 40

Bachrach, Peter, 9, 10
Banfield, Edward, 7, 27
Baratz, Morton, 9, 10
Becker, Carl, 2n
Benson, George, 2n
Brazer, Harvey, 8
Bryce, James, 2n

Clark, Jane, 2n, 18
Clark, Terry, 8
Cole, Richard, 4n, 114n
Corwin, Edward, 2n

Dahl, Robert, 9
Davis, David, 2n, 3n, 27
Donovan, John, 4n
Drucker, Peter, 27, 28
Dye, Thomas, 8, 17

Eckfield, Richard, 52
Elazar, Danier, 2n, 3

Farkas, Suzanne, 11, 33
Field, John, 7, 129
Fowler, Edmund, 7, 171

Goodwin, Richard, 27-28
Grodzins, Morton, 2, 3

Hawkins, Brett, 8
Healy, Patrick, 107
Heilbroner, Robert, 17
Heller, Walter, 25, 26, 60, 106

Hoffstadter, Richard, 7
Holcombe, Arthur, 2n
Hunter, Floyd, 9

Levitan, Sar, 4n
Lineberry, Robert, 7, 171
Lynd, Helen, 9
Lynd, Robert, 9

McBreen, Maureen, 5n, 17n, 18
Moynihan, Daniel, 4n, 27

Nathan, Richard, 30, 59-60

Polsby, Nelson, 9n

Reagan, Michael, 2n, 31
Reuss, Henry, 22, 24, 67
Riker, William, 2n

Scammon, Richard, 123n
Schattschneider, E.E., 9, 10, 31, 153
Stephens, Alexander, 2n
Strange, John, 114
Sundquist, James, 2n, 3n, 27

Thompson, Richard, 40, 46

Walker, Jack, 9
Watt, Graham, 150
Wattenberg, Ben, 123n
Watson, John, 9n
Williams, Austin, 121n
Wilson, James, 7
Wolfinger, Raymond, 7, 129

Subject Index

accountability, 4-5
Advisory Commission on Intergovern-
mental Relations, 21, 30
AFL-CIO, 45
American Civil Liberties Union, 45-46
American Federation of State, County,
and Municipal Employees, 45
Ashley, Thomas L., 41
assessment of general revenue sharing,
153-156

Bachrach, Peter, 9-10
Baker, Howard, 30, 41
Banfield, Edward, 7, 27
Baratz, Morton S., 9-10
Beggs, James, 58
Biemiller, Andrew J., 45
block grants, 122
block grants plan, 31
Brazer, Harvey E., 8
Brookings Institution, 68
Buckley, James, 50
Burns, Arthur, 30

categorical grants, 10-11, 18-19, 31, 61
Center for Community Change, 68
centrist critics, 27-28
Civil War, 2
Clark, Jane, 18
Clark, Terry W., 8
coalition politics, 141-145
Community Action Agencies, 103, 108
community power, 9-10
compliance complaints, 151-153
Comprehensive Employment and
Training Act, 58
Congressional elections, November,
1974, 124
Connally, John, 43
consequences of general revenue shar-
ing, 148-149
Constitution, 3
Council of State Governments, 46

Dahl, Robert, 9
Davis, David, 27
decentralization, 6-10
Drucker, Peter F., 27-28
Dye, Thomas, 8, 17

Eckfield, Richard, 52
Economic Opportunity Act, 4
Ehrlichman, John, 44
Elazar, Daniel, 3
environmental variables, 8-9
evaluation of general revenue sharing,
153-156
executive branch reorganization, 59

Farkas, Suzanne, 11, 33
federalism, 2-3, 5-6
federal regional councils, 53
Field, John Osgood, 7, 129
"fiscal crises," 114
fiscal crisis of 1950-1972, 19-22
Ford, Gerald, 121, 144
Fountain, H.L., 67, 123
Fowler, Edmund P., 7
fungibility, 68-69

Gallup Poll, 29
general revenue sharing: additive versus substitution positions, 60-61;
and categorical grant programs,
103-105; and future questions,
121; and innovation, 154; and
municipal officials attitudes,
108-112; and property taxes, 154;
community power debate, 10-11;
distribution of funds, 48-49; expenditure summary, 90; expenditures and citizen participation,
98-103; expenditures compared
with prior budgetary year, 70-73;
expenditures and demographic
variables, 84-90; expenditures
and effect of political and en-

177

vironmental characteristics,
112-116; expenditures and empirical results, 147-150; expenditures and municipal reform, 80-84; expenditures and region, 76, 78-79; expenditures and size, 73-76; expenditures and type of city, 76-77; funds received by 50 largest cities, 1973, 56-57; funds received by 50 states, 1973, 54-55; history of, 17-33; House of Representatives debate, 43-46; legislation, 155; locus of decision-making, 33; New Federalism, 39; 1971 State of the Union Address, 42; recipient satisfaction, 124-140; restrictions, 169-170; revised Nixon plan, 42-43; tax efforts, 105-108; tax relief aspects, 107
Goodell, Charles E., 23, 41
Goodwin, Richard, 27-28
governmental structure and support of general revenue sharing, 125-129
grant-in-aid programs, 11, 150
Grodzins, Morton, 2-3

Hatcher, Richard, 99-100
Hawkins, Brett W., 8
Healy, Patrick, 107
Heilbroner, Robert, 17
Heller, Walter, 25-27, 60-61, 106
Heller-Pechman Proposal, 30
Highway Trust fund, 53
Hofstadter, Richard C., 7
House Appropriations Committee, 43
House of Representatives, 70, 124, 145
House Ways and Means Committee, 43, 46-47, 104
Housing Act of 1949, 3
Hunter, Floyd, 9

impact of general revenue sharing, 148-150
innovation and revenue sharing, 95-98
Intergovernmental Fiscal Coordination Act of 1971, 47

International City Management Association, 46

Jackson, Andrew, 17
Jackson, Henry, 123
Jackson, Jesse, Rev., 99
Javits, Jacob, 104
Johnson, Lyndon B., 23, 26-27
Joint Committee on Internal Revenue Taxation, 47

Kennedy, John F., 27
Kennedy, T., 123

Laird, Melvin, 22-23
Landrieu, Moon, 61, 122-124
"layer cake" theory, 2
League of Women Voters, 73
League of Women Voters Education Fund, 68
Legislative Action Committee, 46
Lineberry, Robert L., 7
Long, Russell, 41
Lugar, Richard, 46
Lynd, Helen M., 9
Lynd, Robert S., 9

Mahon, George, 43-44, 49
Maier, Henry, 109
"marble cake theory," 2
Martin, John, 47
matching funds prohibition, 4
maximum feasible participation, 4
McBreen, Maureen, 18
mean income, 84-86
Mills, Wilbur, 5, 41-47
Mineta, Norman, 104
mobilization of bias, 9-10
Model Cities, 61, 99, 103-105, 108, 114-115, 149, 153
Model Cities funds, 72
Morrill Act, 18
Mosher, E.A., 46
Moynihan, Daniel, 27
municipal official's attitudes, 108-112
Muskie, Edmund, 41, 108, 123

Nathan, Richard, 29-30, 59-61
Nathan Task Force, 29-30
National Association for the Advancement of Colored People, 46
National Association of Counties, 46
National Governors' Conference, 46
National League of Cities, 46, 107, 122
National Legislative Conference, 46
National Planning Association, 67
National Science Foundation, 67
National Urban Coalition, 68
Nelson, Gaylord, 104
New Deal, 40
"New Federalism," 30, 53-61, 104; opposition views, 40-41, 60-61
Nixon, Richard M., 10, 29, 39-40, 42-43, 47, 53, 56, 58-59, 95-96, 99, 103, 107-109, 122-124
non-issues and community power, 9-10
non-white population and general revenue sharing expenditures, 86-88

Office of Economic Opportunity, 99, 103-105, 114-115, 148, 150, 153
Office of Revenue Sharing, 67, 73, 147, 151-152

Pechman, Joseph A., 27
pluralist thought, 9
policy analysts, 150
policy innovation, 150
policy outcomes, 9-10
political ethos, 7-8
population change and general revenue sharing expenditures, 88-89
priority expenditures, 52, 67
property taxes, 21
public hearings and general revenue sharing decisions, 101-103
public interest, 31

questionnaires, 161-168

Reagan, Michael, 31
reform cities and general revenue sharing, 80-84

reform governments and innovation, 96-97
reform scale, 171
regional councils, 59
renewal legislation, 142-145
Republican Party Platform of 1968, 29
response rates, 68-69
Reuss, Henry, 22, 24, 123
revenue sharing: Goodell proposal, 23; Heller proposal, 25-27; Laird proposal, 22-23; Pechman Report, 27; Republican Coordinating Committee proposal, 23; Reuss proposal, 24. See general revenue sharing
Ribicoff, Abraham, 50
rural community development, 58-59

sales taxes, 21
Schattschneider, E.E., 9-10, 31
Senate Finance Committee, 50
Senate Government Operations Subcommittee on Intergovernmental Relations, 41, 59-60, 104, 108, 122
"shared" functions, 2
Shultz, George, 49
social services, 155
special revenue sharing, 53, 58, 122
State and Local Fiscal Assistance Act of 1972, 6-8, 48-49, 51-52
State of the Union Address, 1971, 59, 95
State of the Union Address, 1972, 96
state income tax, 20
Stokes, Carl, 46
Strange, John, 114
Sundquist, James, 27
Surplus Distribution Act of 1836, 17-18

tax credit plan, 30
Tenth Amendment, 3
theoretical aspects of general revenue sharing, 150-153
Thompson, Richard, 40-41
transportation revenue sharing, 58-59

Uhlman, Wesley, 108

United States Conference of Mayors, 46
urban renewal funds, 72

Walker, Jack, 9
War on Poverty, 3-5
Watergate, 123-124

Watt, Graham, 151
Weidenbaum, Murray L., 30
White, Kevin, 74, 109
Wilson, James Q., 7
Wolfinger, Raymond, 7, 129
Woodworth, Lawrence, 47

About the Authors

David A. Caputo received the B.A. from Miami University and the M.A. M.Phil., and Ph.D. degrees from Yale University. He is currently associate professor of political science at Purdue University where he teaches courses in urban politics, intergovernmental relations, and public policy. He is the author of *American Politics and Public Policy: An Introduction* (J.B. Lippincott, 1974), and several monographs and book chapters dealing with organized crime, population policy, and urban politics. He has contributed to the *Public Administration Review,* the *Midwest Journal of Political Science, 1974 Municipal Year Book, Publius, Tax Review,* and *Urban Affairs Quarterly.*

Richard L. Cole received the B.A. and M.A. from North Texas State University and the Ph.D. from Purdue University. He is currently assistant professor of political science at George Washington University where he teaches courses in urban politics, state politics, and political methodology. He is the author of *Citizen Participation and the Urban Policy Process* (Lexington Books, 1974). He has contributed to the *Midwest Journal of Political Science, 1974 Municipal Year Book, Publius, Social Science Quarterly, Tax Review,* and *Urban Affairs Quarterly.*